I0020170

Code:
3 Books in 1

*Advanced Guide to
Programming Code
with Python*

*Advanced Guide to
Programming Code
with JavaScript*

*Advanced Guide to
Programming Code
with Java*

Charlie Masterson

Table of Contents

Java: Advanced Guide to Programming Code with Java

About this Bundle:

Congratulations on owning *Code: 3 Books in 1 – Advanced Guide to Programming Code with Python+JavaScript+Java* and thanks for doing so.

What you are about to read is a collection of three separate books on how to learn Python, JavaScript and Java computer programming.

Each book will discuss learning Python, JavaScript and Java from an advanced level.

Book 1:
<u>Python: Advanced Guide to Programming Code with Python</u>

Here you will learn the basic essentials of learning Python – the necessary topics you require in gaining advanced level knowledge.

Book 2:
<u>JavaScript: Advanced Guide to Programming Code with JavaScript</u>

Here you will learn the advanced essentials of learning JavaScript – the necessary topics you require in gaining advanced level knowledge.

Book 3:
Java: Advanced Guide to Programming Code with Java

Here you will learn the advanced essentials of learning Java – the necessary topics you require in gaining advanced level knowledge.

Thanks again for owning this book!

Let us begin with the first book in the Code bundle:

Python:

Advanced Guide to Programming Code with Python

Charlie Masterson

Introduction

I want to thank you and congratulate you for downloading the book, *"Python: Advanced Guide to Programming Code with Python"*.

This book contains advanced steps and strategies on how to further your Python programming knowledge.

This book is exactly what the title says – advanced so, if you have little to no knowledge of programming with Python, this really isn't the book for you. It is aimed at those who are competent at basic Python programming and want to further their knowledge by learning some of the more advanced concepts but this is by no means a comprehensive guide to all the advanced programming concepts. Instead I have picked some of the more important ones that you should learn and I hope that you gain something from reading this and working through the code examples.

Thanks again for downloading this book, I hope you enjoy it!

Chapter 1: Python Comprehensions

Once you get to know a list comprehension, once you get what they are, you will find that they become quite compelling. So, what is a Python comprehension? Basically, they are constructs that let a sequence be built from another sequence. Python 2.0 introduced list comprehensions while Python 3.0 continues with set and dictionary comprehensions.

List Comprehensions

A list comprehension is made up of the following components:

- Input sequence
- Variable that represents the members of that input sequence
- Optional predicate expression
- Output expression – this satisfies the predicate by taking the input sequence members and producing the elements of the output list

Let's say that you want a list of the integers that are in a sequence and then you want to square them:

Example codes:

```
a_list = [1, '4', 9, 'a', 0, 4]
```

```
squared_ints = [ e**2 for e in a_list if
type(e) == types.IntType ]

print squared_ints
# [ 1, 81, 0, 16 ]
```

Here's how that works:

- The iterator part of the statement will iterate through each individual member if the input sequence known as a_list
- The predicate will then check to see if each one is an integer
- If it is, it will be passed to the output expression and then squared, becoming a member in the output list

You can get pretty much the same result if you use the Python built-in functions, filter and map or the lambda function:

The map function will modify the members in the sequence:

```
map(lambda e: e**2, a_list)
```

While the filter function will apply a predicate to the sequence:

```
filter(lambda      e:      type(e)      ==
types.IntType, a_list)
```

You can combine these:

```
map(lambda   e:   e**2,   filter(lambda   e:
type(e) == types.IntType, a_list))
```

Ok, so this example is showing you three function calls – *map*, *type* and *filter* – and two calls to *lambda*. Just be aware that Python function calls can be expensive and note that the input sequence has been traversed twice and filter is what produces an intermediate list.

List comprehensions are enclosed in lists so it is very easy to see that a list has been produced. You don't need any call to lambda and only one to type; instead, list comprehensions use iterators, which we will talk about more in the next chapter, as well as an expression and, if you use the optional predicate, an if expression.

Nested Comprehensions

Take an identity matrix, size n. That is a square matrix of n by n and the ones will be listed on the main diagonal.

A 3 by 3 example of that is:

1	0	0
0	1	0
0	0	1

In Python, we would represent this matrix by using a list of lists. Each of the sub-lists is representative of a row and a 3 by 3 matrix would be shown by way of this code:

```
[ [ 1, 0, 0 ],
  [ 0, 1, 0 ],
  [ 0, 0, 1 ] ]
```

To generate this matrix, we would use this comprehension:

```
[ [ 1 if item_idx == row_idx else 0 for
item_idx in range(0, 3) ] for row_idx in
range(0, 3) ]
```

Techniques

By using zip() you can deal with at least two elements at any one time:

```
['%s=%s' % (n, v) for n, v in
zip(self.all_names, self)]
```

To automatically unpack a tuple, you can use multiple types:

```
[f(v) for (n, f), v in
zip(cls.all_slots, values)]
```

You can use os.walk() for a two-level list comprehension:

```
# Comprehensions/os_walk_comprehension.py
import os
```

```
restFiles = [os.path.join(d[0], f) for d
in os.walk(".")
            for   f   in   d[2]   if
f.endswith(".rst")]
for r in restFiles:
    print(r)
```

A more complicated example of that will give you a description of all of the parts:

```
# CodeManager.py
"""
TODO: Break the check into two pieces?
TODO:  update()  this  is  still  in  test
mode;  it  doesn't  actually  work  properly
yet.
```

Another way of doing this would be to place the codeMarker and the first line (which should be indented) into the restructures text file and then you can run the update program, which will insert the rest automatically:

```
CODE:

"""
import  os,  re,  sys,  shutil,  inspect,
difflib

restFiles = [os.path.join(d[0], f) for d
in os.walk(".") if not "_test" in d[0]
            for   f   in   d[2]   if
f.endswith(".rst")]
Classes
class Python:
        codeMarker = "::\n\n"
```

```
        commentTag = "#"
        listings   =   re.compile("::\n\n(
{4}#.*(?:\n+ {4}.*)*)")
class Java:
        codeMarker  =  "..    code-block::
java\n\n"
        commentTag = "//"
        listings = \
            re.compile("..    *code-block::
*java\n\n( {4}//.*(?:\n+ {4}.*)*)")
```

def shift(name of listing):

```
    "this  will  move  the  listing  to  the
left by 4 spaces"
    return [x[4:] if x.startswith("    ")
else x for x in listing.splitlines()]

# TEST - this makes duplicates of all the
.rst files that are in a test directory
to test update():
dirs     =     set([os.path.join("_test",
os.path.dirname(f)) for f in restFiles])
if [os.makedirs(d) for d in dirs if not
os.path.exists(d)]:
    [shutil.copy(f,  os.path.join("_test",
f)) for f in restFiles]
testFiles = [os.path.join(d[0], f) for d
in os.walk("_test")
            for   f   in   d[2]    if
f.endswith(".rst")]
```

class Commands:

```
    """
Each of the static methods is able to be
called from the command line so you would
```

```
add in a new static method at this point
to add a new command into the program
    """


    @staticmethod
    def display(language):
        """
        Print all of the code listings
that are in the .rst files.
        """
        for f in restFiles:
            listings                    =
language.listings.findall(open(f).read())
            if not listings: continue
            print('=' * 60 + "\n" + f +
"\n" + '=' * 60)
                for       n,       l       in
enumerate(listings):

print("\n".join(shift(l)))
                if n < len(listings) - 1:
                    print('-' * 60)


    @staticmethod
```

def extract(name of language):

```
        """
Pull all of the code listings from the
.rst files and then write each one into
its own file. This will not overwrite in
the event that the .rst files and the
code files do not agree unless you insert
"extract -force"
        """
        force = len(sys.argv) == 3 and
sys.argv[2] == '-force'
        paths = set()
```

```python
        for listing in [shift(listing)
for f in restFiles
                for listing in
language.listings.findall(open(f).read())
]:
            path =
listing[0][len(language.commentTag):].str
ip()
            if path in paths:
                print("ERROR: Duplicate
file name: %s" % path)
                sys.exit(1)
            else:
                paths.add(path)
            path = os.path.join("..",
"code", path)
            dirname =
os.path.dirname(path)
            if dirname and not
os.path.exists(dirname):
                os.makedirs(dirname)
            if os.path.exists(path) and
not force:
                for i in
difflib.ndiff(open(path).read().splitline
s(), listing):
                    if i.startswith("+ ")
or i.startswith("- "):
                        print("ERROR:
Existing file different from .rst")
                        print("Use
'extract -force' to force overwrite")

Commands.check(language)
                    return
            file(path,
'w').write("\n".join(listing))
```

```python
    @staticmethod
    def check(name of language):
        """
        Make sure that all the external
        code files exist and then check which of
        the external files have changed the
        contents of the .rst files. This
        generates files in the subdirectory
        called _deltas to show what changes have
        been made
        """
        class Result: # Messenger
            def __init__(self, **kwargs):
                self.__dict__ = kwargs
        result = Result(missing = [],
deltas = [])
        listings = [Result(code =
shift(code), file = f)
                for f in restFiles
for code in

language.listings.findall(open(f).read())
]
        paths =
[os.path.normpath(os.path.join("..",
"code", path)) for path in

[listing.code[0].strip()[len(language.com
mentTag):].strip()
                for listing in
listings]]
        if os.path.exists("_deltas"):
            shutil.rmtree("_deltas")
        for path, listing in zip(paths,
listings):
            if not os.path.exists(path):
```

```python
                result.missing.append(path)
            else:
                code                    =
open(path).read().splitlines()
                for         i           in
difflib.ndiff(listing.code, code):
                    if i.startswith("+ ")
or i.startswith("- "):
                        d                =
difflib.HtmlDiff()
                        if              not
os.path.exists("_deltas"):

os.makedirs("_deltas")
                        html             =
os.path.join("_deltas",

os.path.basename(path).split('.')[0]     +
".html")
                        open(html,
'w').write(

"<html><h1>Left: %s<br>Right: %s</h1>" %

(listing.file, path) +

d.make_file(listing.code, code))

result.deltas.append(Result(file           =
listing.file,
                            path = path,
html = html, code = code))
                        break
        if result.missing:
            print("Missing %s files:\n%s"
%
```

```
                      (language.__name__,
"\n".join(result.missing)))
        for delta in result.deltas:
            print("%s changed in %s; see
%s" %
                      (delta.file,
delta.path, delta.html))
        return result

    @staticmethod
```

def update(name of language): *# Test until this is deemed trustworthy*

```
        """
        Refresh the external code files
into .rst files.
        """
        check_result                =
Commands.check(language)
        if check_result.missing:
            print(language.__name__,
"update aborted")
            return
        changed = False
        def _update(matchobj):
            listing                  =
shift(matchobj.group(1))
            path                      =
listing[0].strip()[len(language.commentTa
g):].strip()
            filename                  =
os.path.basename(path).split('.')[0]
            path    =    os.path.join("..",
"code", path)
            code                      =
open(path).read().splitlines()
```

```
            return  language.codeMarker  +
\
                "\n".join([("            "  +
line).rstrip() for line in listing])
        for f in testFiles:
            updated                 =
language.listings.sub(_update,
open(f).read())
            open(f, 'w').write(updated)

if __name__ == "__main__":
    commands                          =
dict(inspect.getmembers(Commands,
inspect.isfunction))
    if len(sys.argv) < 2 or sys.argv[1]
not in commands:
        print("Command line options:\n")
        for name in commands:
            print(name    +    ":    "    +
commands[name].__doc__)
    else:
        for           language           in
inspect.getmembers(Languages,
inspect.isclass):

commands[sys.argv[1]](language[1])
```

Set Comprehensions

A set comprehension helps you to construct
sets with the exact same principles as the list
comprehension with just one difference – the
result is a set, not a list. Let's say that you have
a list of names; this list can contain those
names that are different from the case that is
used to represent them, which are duplicates

and those that contain just one character. The names that we want are those that are longer than a single character and we want to represent all of the names in the same format. For this, all the first letters have to be capitalized while all other letters are lower case.

This is the list that you begin with:

```
names = [ 'Billy', 'JASON', 'alison',
'billy', 'ALISON', 'J', 'Billy' ]
The set that we want is:
{ 'Billy', 'Jason', 'Alison' }
```

Did you spot the new syntax used to denote a set? We enclose the members of the set inside curly braces {} and the following example shows you a set comprehension that does this:

```
{ name[0].upper() + name[1:].lower() for
name in names if len(name) > 1 }
```

Dictionary Comprehensions

Let's say that you have a dictionary and the keys in it are characters. The values of those characters' map to how often the character appears in the text and the dictionary are able to determine the difference between lower and upper case characters.

What we want is a dictionary that combines the occurrences of lower and upper case characters and this is how you do it:

CODE:

```
mcase = {'a':10, 'b': 34, 'A': 7, 'Z':3}

mcase_frequency    =    {    k.lower()    :
mcase.get(k.lower(),         0)           +
mcase.get(k.upper(),    0)    for    k    in
mcase.keys()  }

#  mcase_frequency  ==  {'a':  17,  'z':  3,
'b': 34}
```

Chapter 2:
Python Iterators

Iterators

Let's begin with iterators. In Python, iterator objects follow the iterator protocol while supporting two different methods. This is a requirement of Python:

- `__iter__` will return the iterator object. We use this in both the *in* and *for* statements
- `__next__` method will return the next value that comes from the iterator. If there are no more values to return, a `StopIteration` exception should be raised.

class Counter(name of object):

```
def __init__(self, low, high):
    self.current = low
    self.high = high

def __iter__(self):
    'Will    return    itself    as    an
iterator object'
    return self

def __next__(self):
    'will  return  the  next  value  from
the  iterator  until  the  current  value  is
lower than high'
    if self.current > self.high:
        raise StopIteration
    else:
```

```
        self.current += 1
        return self.current - 1
```

This iterator can now be used in the code:

```
>>> c = Counter(1,5)
>>> for i in c:
...     print(i, end=' ')
...
1 2 3 4 5
```

Don't forget; we can only use an iterator object one single time and that means that, once *StopIteration* has been raised once, the same exception will keep on being raised

```
>>> c = Counter(2,3)
>>> next(c)
2
>>> next(c)
3
>>> next(c)
Traceback (the most recent call last):
File "<stdin>", line 1, in <module>
File "<stdin>", line 11, in next
StopIteration
>>> next(c)
Traceback (the most recent call last):
File "<stdin>", line 1, in <module>
File "<stdin>", line 11, in next
StopIteration
```

If you use the iterator in the *for* loop, the next example will try to show what the code is behind the scenes:

```
>>> iterator = iter(c)
>>> while True:
...     try:
...         x = iterator.__next__()
...         print(x, end=' ')
...     except StopIteration as e:
...         break
...
1 2 3 4 5
```

Chapter 3: Python Generators

Now we look at Python generators, first introduced with Python v2.3. Generators are a much easier way of creating iterators from a function by using the keyword *yield:*

```
>>> def my_generator():
...       print("Inside my generator")
...       yield 'a'
...       yield 'b'
...       yield 'c'
...
>>> my_generator()
<generator    object    my_generator    at
0x7fbcfa0a6aa0>
```

So, in this example, we created a very simple generator by using the `yield` statements and, like any other iterator, you can use it in a `for` loop:

```
>>> for char in my_generator():
...       print(char)
...
Inside the generator
a
b
c
```

Here is another example where we create the `Counter` class through the use of a generator function and then we use it inside a `for` loop:

```
def counter_generator(low, high):
    while low <= high:
```

```
        yield low
        low += 1

>>> for i in counter_generator(1,5):
...         print(i, end=' ')
...
1 2 3 4 5
```

When the `while` loop gets to the `yield`
statement, inside the loop you will notice that
the return is a value of low and generator state
becomes suspended. Now look at the second
`next` call; the generator has resumed from
where it stopped before and the value is
increased by one. The `while` loop will continue
round to the `yield` statement.

When you call generator functions, they return
generator objects so, if you were to call *dir*
on the object you would find that it has the
__next__ and the __iter__ methods
included, along with some other methods:

```
>>> c = counter_generator(1,5)
>>> dir(c)
['__class__',                '__delattr__',
'__dir__',      '__doc__',          '__eq__',
'__format__',
'__ge__',   '__getattribute__',    '__gt__',
'__hash__', '__init__', '__iter__',
'__le__', '__lt__', '__name__', '__ne__',
'__new__', '__next__', '__reduce__',
'__reduce_ex__',                   '__repr__',
'__setattr__', '__sizeof__', '__str__',
'__subclasshook__',
```

```
'close',        'gi_code',        'gi_frame',
'gi_running', 'send', 'throw']
```

We tend to use generators as a way of making lazy evaluations and, in this way, they become one of the best approaches when you are working with a lot of data. If you don't want to go down the route of loading all of your data into memory, a generator can be used to pass you the data one piece at a time.

Perhaps the biggest and best example of this is the function *os.path.walk()*. This will use a callback function together with the *os.walk* generator. Using this generator will save a ton of memory. There are generators which can produce infinite values and this is an example of one:

```
>>> def infinite_generator(start=0):
...       while True:
...           yield start
...           start += 1
...
>>> for num in infinite_generator(1):
...       print(num, end=' ')
...       if num > 15:
...           break
...
1 2 3 4 5 6 7 8 9 10 11 12 13 14 15 16
```

If we were to go back to the *my_generator* example you would find out one thing about

generators — they cannot be re-used.
Remember, we said they are single use only:

```
>>> g = my_generator()
>>> for c in g:
...         print(c)
...
Inside my_generator you would see
a
b
c
>>> for c in g:
...         print(c)
...
```

There is a way to create a generator that can be reused and that is to use a generator that is Object-based because these do not hold a state. Any class that contains an __iter method that yields data may be used as an object generator and, in the following example, we will create the Counter generator:

```
>>> class Counter(object):
...         def __init__(self, low, high):
...             self.low = low
...             self.high = high
...         def __iter__(self):
...             counter = self.low
...             while self.high >= counter:
...                 yield counter
...                 counter += 1
...
>>> gobj = Counter(1, 5)
>>> for num in gobj:
...         print(num, end=' ')
```

```
...
1 2 3 4 5
>>> for num in gobj:
...     print(num, end=' ')
...
1 2 3 4 5
```

Generator Expressions

Generator expressions are a way of generalizing generators and list comprehensions in a memory-efficient and high-performance way. In this next example, we are going to try summing up the squares of all numbers between 1 and 9:

```
>>> sum([x*x for x in range(1,10)])
```

What we have done here is create a list that contains the square values in memory. We then iterate over the list and, after the sum, the memory is freed. This is better understood where you have a bigger list. The generator expression can be used to save memory:

```
sum(x*x for x in range(1,10))
```

The syntax that we use for the generator expression dictates that it must always be directly within parentheses and must not contain a comma either side of it. This means that either of the examples below can be used as valid generator expressions:

```
>>> sum(x*x for x in range(1,10))
285
>>> g = (x*x for x in range(1,10))
>>> g
<generator     object     <genexpr>     at
0x7fc559516b90>
```

You can chain generators or generator expressions and, with the following example, we are going to read a file called */var/log/cron*. We are looking to see if there are any specific jobs that are running successfully or not – we are looking for one called anacron. You can also achieve the same with the shell command *tail -f /var/log/cron |grep anacron*

```
>>> jobtext = 'anacron'
>>>    all    =    (line    for    line    in
open('/var/log/cron', 'r') )
>>> job = ( line for line in all if
line.find(jobtext) != -1)
>>> text = next(job)
>>> text
"May        6    12:17:15    dhcp193-104
anacron[23052]:     Job     `cron.daily'
terminated\n"
>>> text = next(job)
>>> text
'May        6    12:17:15    dhcp193-104
anacron[23052]:    Normal    exit    (1    job
run)\n'
>>> text = next(job)
>>> text
```

'May   6   13:01:01   dhcp193-104   run-
parts(/etc/cron.hourly)[25907]:   starting
0anacron\n

Chapter 4:
Python
Decorators

Decorators give us a way of calling higher-order functions by using a much simpler syntax. The definition of a Python decorator is "a function that takes another function and then extends the behavior of the last function without explicit modification". That probably sounds incredibly confusing but, really, it isn't and you will see that through the following examples:

Example 1:

```
def my_decorator(some_function):

    def wrapper():

        print("Something happens before we call
            some_function()")

        some_function()

        print("Something happens after we call
            some_function()")

    return wrapper


def just_some_function():
    print("Whee!")


just_some_function =
my_decorator(just_some_function)

just_some_function()
```

Have a guess at what the output of this code is going to be. I'll give you a couple of clues – something happens before we call `some_function` and then something happens after we call `some_function`

Simply put, a decorator wraps a function and modifies the behavior of the function. Let's add in an *if* statement:

Example 2:

```
def my_decorator(some_function):

    def wrapper():

        num = 10

        if num == 10:
            print("Yes!")
        else:
            print("No!")

        some_function()

        print("Something happens after we
call some_function()")

    return wrapper


def just_some_function():
    print("Whee!")
```

```
just_some_function                    =
my_decorator(just_some_function)

just_some_function()
```

The result of this is the output:

```
Yes!
Whee!
Something    happens    after    we    call
some_function().
```

Python lets you use the "pie" syntax (the @ symbol) to make calling a decorator much simpler.

Next, we are going to create a module for the decorator:

```
def my_decorator(some_function):

    def wrapper():

        num = 10

        if num == 10:
            print("Yes!")
        else:
            print("No!")

        some_function()

        print("Something happens after we
call some_function() .")

    return wrapper
```

```
if __name__ == "__main__":
    my_decorator()
```

Okay, still with me? Hang on there because all will become clear. Now we are going to call the function using the decorator:

```
from decorator07 import my_decorator

@my_decorator
def just_some_function():
    print("Whee!")

just_some_function()
```

When this example is run, the output should be exactly the same as the last one:

```
Yes!
Whee!
Something    happens    after    we    call
some_function().
```

So, using `@my_decorator` is a much better and easier way of saying `just_some_function = my_decorator(just_some_function)` and this is the way that a decorator is applied to a function.

Let's look at a few real-world examples:

```
CODE:
```

```python
import time

def timing_function(some_function):

    """
    Will outputs the time that a function takes
    to execute.
    """

    def wrapper():
        t1 = time.time()
        some_function()
        t2 = time.time()
        return "Time it took to run the function: " + str((t2 - t1)) + "\n"
    return wrapper


@timing_function
def my_function():
    num_list = []
    for num in (range(0, 10000)):
        num_list.append(num)
    print("\nSum of all the numbers: " + str((sum(num_list))))


print(my_function())
```

The output will be the time before `my_function()` was run and the time after it. The next step is to subtract one number from the other to get the time taken to run the function

Have a good look at it; run the code and work through it, one line at a time and ensure that you fully understand how it all works:

```python
from time import sleep


def sleep_decorator(function):

    """
    This limits how fast the function may be
    called.
    """

    def wrapper(*args, **kwargs):
        sleep(2)
        return function(*args, **kwargs)
    return wrapper


@sleep_decorator
def print_number(num):
    return num

print(print_number(222))

for num in range(1, 6):
    print(print_number(num))
```

We use this decorator for rate limiting – test it out and see what happens.

One of the most popular of all the Python decorators is `login_required()`. This makes sure that a person is logged in or authenticated properly before a specific route can be accessed, in this case /secret:

```
from functools import wraps
from flask import g, request, redirect,
url_for


def login_required(f):
    @wraps(f)
    def            decorated_function(*args,
**kwargs):
        if g.user is None:
            return
redirect(url_for('login',
next=request.url))
        return f(*args, **kwargs)
    return decorated_function


@app.route('/secret')
@login_required
def secret():
    pass
```

What did you notice about this? Did you spot that the function has been passed back to the decorator functools.wraps()?

One last example: this is a Flask route handler:

```
@app.route('/grade', methods=['POST'])
def update_grade():
    json_data = request.get_json()
    if 'student_id' not in json_data:
        abort(400)
```

```
    # update database
    return "success!"
```

Here, we are making sure that the key called student_id is made a part of the request. While this does work, the validation really doesn't belong in the function. As well as that, there are other routes that may use the same validations so we use a decorator to take out any logic that is unnecessary:

```
from flask import Flask, request, abort
from functools import wraps

app = Flask(__name__)


def validate_json(*expected_args):
    def decorator(func):
        @wraps(func)
        def wrapper(*args, **kwargs):
            json_object              =
request.get_json()
            for        expected_arg        in
expected_args:
                if  expected_arg  not  in
json_object:
                    abort(400)
            return func(*args, **kwargs)
        return wrapper
    return decorator

@app.route('/grade', methods=['POST'])
@validate_json('student_id')
def update_grade():
    json_data = request.get_json()
```

```
print(json_data)
# update database
return "success!"
```

In this code, the decorator has taken a variable length list and used it as an argument and that lets us pass in whatever string arguments are necessary, as many as it takes. Each one will represent a key that is used in validating the JSON data.

One last thing before we leave this chapter — notice anything about that? New decorators are dynamically created based on the strings.

Chapter 5:
Python Context
Managers

Next to decorators, the Python Context Managers are the most common of all the constructs. And, like the decorators they are one of the things that you will use but probably won't truly understand how they work. As any school child will tell you, the easiest way to open a file and read from it is:

```
with
open('what_are_context_managers.txt',
'r') as infile:
    for line in infile:
        print('> {}'.format(line))
```

The thing is, how many of you who handle file input and output (IO) properly know why it is the right way to handle it? Do you even now that there is a wrong way? Hopefully most of you otherwise this will all be a waste of time! But what do we use a context manager for?

Resource Management

Probably the most important, and the most common, use of a context manager is to manage resources properly. In fact, there is a good reason why a context manager is used when we read from a file. When we open a file, the very act of doing so uses a resource known as a file descriptor and your operating system limits this resource. By that, I mean that a process can only open up to a specific number of files at any one time. To prove the point, have a go at running this piece of code:

```
files = []
for x in range(100000):
    files.append(open('foo.txt', 'w'))
```

If you use a Linux or Mac OS computer, you will most likely see an error message that is similar to this one:

```
> python test.py
Traceback (the most recent call last):
  File "test.py", line 3, in <module>
OSError: [Errno 24] Too many open files:
'foo.txt'
```

If you are using Windows it might not be a good idea to try this; if you do, your computer will likely crash and your motherboard burst into flames! The lesson here is, do not leak a file descriptor!

All joking to one side (that won't really happen to your computer), the next question you should be asking is, "What is a file descriptor"? and then you should be asking what it means to "leak" a file descriptor. Let me try to explain – when a file is opened, the operating system will assign an integer to it and this lets it give you access to the file, instead, following direct access to the underlying file. This is good for several reasons, one of which being that you can pass references to the files between the processes. You can also maintain a certain security level that will be enforced by the kernel.

So, how do you "leak" one of these file descriptors? It's simple; when you open a file, you should always close it. If you don't, the file descriptor will leak. It is very easy to forget that you have files open, especially if you are working with several at once but, if you forget to close one, you will soon learn that there is normally a limit to how many file descriptors can be assigned to a process.

On a UNIX system or similar, typing `$ ulimit -n` at the command prompt should tell you what the value of the top limit is, but if you want to see more proof, run the example code above again but replace the number 100000 with whatever number came up when you ran `$ ulimit -n` less about 5, which will account for the files that are opened on startup by the Python interpreter. The code should now run through to completing.

Naturally, as always with Python, there is a much better and simpler way to make your program compete – make sure you close all of your open files. Here is a somewhat elaborate example of how you can fix the issue:

```
files = []
for x in range(10000):
    f = open('foo.txt', 'w')
    f.close()
    files.append(f)
```

An Even Better Way to Manage Your Resources

Of course, in a real system, it isn't all that easy to ensure that you call `close()` of every file that you open, especially if said file is inside a function that could cause an exception or that has a number of return paths. In a more complicated function that can open a file, how could you be expected to remember that you have to add `close()` to all of the places that a function can be returned from? And that is not including all of the exceptions which can come from anywhere. In short, you can't remember and neither can you be expected to.

In other computer programming languages, developers are forced into using `try…except…finally` every single time they work with files or any resource that has to be closed. Luckily, with Python, things are so much easier and we have a very simple way to ensure that all of the resources we have used are cleaned up properly, regardless of whether the code returns a result or if exceptions are thrown up – that solution is a context manager.

Things should be starting to look a little obvious by now. We need to find a convenient method that indicates a specific variable has a cleanup process associated with it. We also need to guarantee that, no matter what happens, the cleanup will happen. So, with that requirement in mind, the syntax that we use for a context manager actually makes a lot of sense:

```
with
something_that_returns_a_context_manager(
) as my_resource:
    do_something(my_resource)
    ...
    print('done using my_resource')
```

That's all there is to it. Using with, you can call anything that can return a context manager, such as the open() function which is built in. You then assign that to a variable by using ...as<variable_name>. The crucial thing to remember here is that the variable will only exist inside the indented block that is underneath the with statement.

It helps if you see the with statement as creating a kind of mini-function; the variable can be used freely inside the indented part but, as soon as that part finishes, the variable will go out of scope. When that happens, a special method is called containing the code that performs the cleanup.

But where, exactly, is that cleanup code? The short answer to that is, the code is wherever the context manager has been defined. There are several ways in which to create a context manager and the simplest way is to define a class containing two methods - __enter__() and __exit__(). The first method will return the resource that is to be managed, and the second method is the one that does the cleanup but doesn't return anything.

To make it all just a little bit clearer, we are going to create a context manager, that is completely redundant, that is for working with files:

```python
class File():

    def __init__(self, filename, mode):
        self.filename = filename
        self.mode = mode

    def __enter__(self):
        self.open_file                    =
open(self.filename, self.mode)
        return self.open_file

    def __exit__(self, *args):
        self.open_file.close()

files = []
for _ in range(10000):
    with File('foo.txt', 'w') as infile:
        infile.write('foo')
```

```
files.append(infile)
```

So, let's look at we have got here. Just like in any class, there is an `__init__ ()` method, responsible for setting up the object. In this case, we have set the file name to open and we have set the mode that it is to be opened up in. `__enter__ ()` opens the file and returns it, at the same time creating `attributeopen_file` — we can now refer to this in `__exit__ ()`.

`__exit__ ()` does nothing more than close the file. When you run the code above, it works because, when the file leaves the with file as `infile: block`, it closes the file. Even if the code within the block raised an exception, that file would still close.

Some More Useful Context Managers

Ok, so given that a context manager is very helpful, it is even more helpful that they have been put into the Standard Library in several different places. Some of the more useful ones are:

- `Lock objects in threading`
- `zipfile.Zipfiles`
- `subProcess.Popen`
- `tarfile.TarFile`
- `telnetib.Telner`
- `Pathlib.Path`

The list goes on forever. Basically, any object that you need to call close on after you have used it is a context manager, or at least, it should be.

One of the more interesting is Lock. In this case, the resource is a mutex and using a context manager stops common deadlock sources from happening in multi-threaded programs. These deadlocks happen when a thread manages to acquire a mutex and will not let go of it. Think about the following example:

from threading import Lock:

```
lock = Lock()

def do_something_dangerous():
    lock.acquire()
    raise Exception('oops I forgot this
code could raise exceptions')
    lock.release()
```

try this:

```
    do_something_dangerous()
except:
    print('Got an exception')
lock.acquire()
print('Got here')
```

It is clear, or it should be that `lock.release()` won't be called and that will cause all of the other threads that call `do_something_dangerous()` to deadlock and, in this example, this is represented by not hitting the line that says `print('Got here')`. We can fix this very easily when we accept and take advantage of Lock being a context manager:

from threading import Lock:

```
lock = Lock()

def do_something_dangerous():
    with lock:
        raise Exception('oops I forgot,
this code is able to raise exceptions')
```

try this:

```
    do_something_dangerous()
except:
    print('Got an exception')
lock.acquire()
print('Got here')
```

Really, there isn't any reasonable way of acquiring Lock through a context manager and then not releasing it and that is exactly as it should be.

Having Fun with `contextlib`

Because context managers are so very useful, there is an entire Standard Library module that is devoted to them and them alone. `contextlib` is full of useful tool for creating context managers and for working with them. One very good shortcut to create a context manager from classes is to use the decorator `@contextmanager`. You use this by decorating a generator function that will call yield only once. Anything that comes before the yield call is considered to be the code for `__enter__()` and everything after is the considered to be the code for `__exit__()`.

Let's rewrite the File context manager with the decorator:

from contextlib import contextmanager:

```
@contextmanager
def open_file(path, mode):
    the_file = open(path, mode)
    yield the_file
    the_file.close()

files = []

for x in range(100000):
    with open_file('foo.txt', 'w') as infile:
        files.append(infile)

for f in files:
    if not f.closed:
        print('not closed')
```

As you see, this is much shorter, only five lines. We have opened the file, we yielded it and then we closed it. The next set of code simply proves that the files have been closed and the other proof is the fact that your program did not crash.

There is a bit of a stupid but fun example that you can find in the official Python.docs but, for the sake of simplicity, here it is:

from contextlib import contextmanager:

```
@contextmanager
def tag(name):
    print("<%s>" % name)
    yield
    print("</%s>" % name)

>>> with tag("h1"):
...     print("foo")
...
<h1>
foo
</h1>
```

The best piece of stupidity and fun with context managers is `contextlib.ContextDecorator` because it allows you to use a class-based approach to defining a context manager while inheriting from `contextlib.ContextDecorator`. By doing this, you are able to use the context manager with the with statement as you would normally or as a function decorator. You could do something similar to the example above by using the following pattern – you shouldn't really do this though because it is just a little bit insane!

from contextlib import ContextDecorator:

```
class makeparagraph(ContextDecorator):
    def __enter__(self):
        print('<p>')
        return self

    def __exit__(self, *exc):
        print('</p>')
        return False

@makeparagraph()
def emit_html():
    print('Here is some non-HTML')

emit_html()
The output will be:
<p>
Here is some non-HTML
</p>
```

Totally useless and just a little horrifying!

Wrapping it Up

By now you should have some idea of what context managers are and how they work, not to mention why they are so useful. As you saw, there are quite a few things that you can do, some useful, some not so useful, with context managers. They have a noble goal in that they make it easier to work with your resources and it makes it much easier to manage created contexts. It's down to you to use these and to make new ones that make life easier for others – just don't make a habit of using them to generate HTML.

Chapter 6: Python Descriptors Overview

Descriptors were first introduced with Python v2.2 and they give us a way of adding a managed attribute to an object. We don't tend to use them in everyday computer programming but you do need to know all about them so that you understand quite a bit of the Python magic that goes on into the third-party packages and the standard library.

The Problem

Let's say that you own and run a bookshop. You use a Python-based inventory management system and that system has a class in it called Book. The class is used to capture the title, the author and the price of all your physical books:

```
    class Book(object):
    def   __init__(self,   author,   title,
price):
        self.author = author
        self.title = title
        self.price = price

    def __str__(self):
        return              "{0}            -
{1}".format(self.author,  self.title)
```

Ok, so this simple class works well for a little while but, sooner or later bad data is going to get into the system. Your system will have loads of books that, because of errors in data entry, will have prices that are too high or even those that are negative. We decide that we want the prices of the books limited to somewhere between 0 and 100. Also, we have a class called Magazine and this has the exact same problem so the solution we come up with must be able to be reused easily.

The Descriptor Protocol

This protocol is nothing more than a set of methods that a class has to implement in order to be qualified as a descriptor. There are three methods:

- `__get__(self, instance, owner)`
- `__set__(self, instance, value)`
- `__delete__(self, instance)`

`__get__` is used to access values that are stored within the object and then return it

`__set__` is used to set a value that is stored within the object and will return nothing

`__delete__` is used to delete a value that is stored within the object and will return nothing

By using all three of these methods, we can create a descriptor that is named Price; this descriptor will place a limit on the stored values of between 0 and 100:

```
from         weakref        import
WeakKeyDictionary
```

```
class Price(object):
    def __init__(self):
        self.default = 0
        self.values = WeakKeyDictionary()

    def __get__(self, instance, owner):
        return   self.values.get(instance,
self.default)

    def __set__(self, instance, value):
        if value < 0 or value > 100:
            raise          ValueError("Price
should be between 0 and 100.")
        self.values[instance] = value

    def __delete__(self, instance):
        del self.values[instance]
```

There are a few things that you need to be
aware of in terms of the Price implementation:

- You must add an instance of any
  descriptor you use to the class and it
  must be a class attribute, not an instance
  attribute. That means, to store the data
  for each instance, the descriptor must
  maintain a dictionary and that
  dictionary must map instances to values
  that are instance-specific. In the Price
  implementation, the dictionary is named
  as self.values

- Python dictionaries will store references
  to the objects that are used as keys and

those references, on their own, are sufficient to stop the object from being garbage collected. When we are finished with the Book instances, to stop them from hanging about we use `WeakKeyDictionary,` from `Weakref` standard module. As soon as the final strong reference passes on, the key pair associated with it will be discarded

Chapter 7:
Using Python
Descriptors

As you have seen, descriptors have a close link to classes and not to instances so, if you want to add a descriptor to the Book class, it has to be added as a class variable, not an instance:

```
class Book(object):
    price = Price()

    def __init__(self, author, title,
price):
        self.author = author
        self.title = title
        self.price = price

    def __str__(self):
        return          "{0}        -
{1}".format(self.author, self.title)
```

We have now enforced a Price constraint for the Books class

```
    >>> b = Book("J K Rowling", "Harry
Potter and the Chamber of Secrets", 12)
>>> b.price
12
>>> b.price = -12
Traceback (most recent call last):
  File    "<pyshell#68>",    line   1,   in
<module>
    b.price = -12
  File "<pyshell#58>", line 9, in __set__
    raise  ValueError("Price   should   be
between 0 and 100.")
ValueError: Price should be between 0 and
100.
>>> b.price = 101
```

```
Traceback (most recent call last):
  File   "<pyshell#69>",   line   1,   in
<module>
    b.price = 101
  File "<pyshell#58>", line 9, in __set__
    raise   ValueError("Price   should   be
between 0 and 100.")
ValueError: Price should be between 0 and
100.
```

How We Access Descriptors

Ok, so we have implemented a fully working descriptor, one that can manage the price attribute for the Book class but it may not be all that clear at this stage how it actually works. It all feels just a little bit like magic but it really isn't. In fact, accessing descriptors is really quite easy:

- When you attempt to evaluate `b.price` and get the value from it, Python will recognize Price as a descriptor and it will call `Book.price.__get__`
- When you attempt to change the price attribute value, for example, `b.price = 22`, Python will, once again, recognize price as a descriptor and will substitute the assignment with the call to `Book.price.__set__`
- And, lastly, when you attempt to delete a price attribute that is stored against a Book instance, Python will automatically

interpret it as the call to
`Book.price.__delete__`

Unless you understand fully that a descriptor is linked to a class and not to an instance, and, as such, have to maintain mapping to instance-specific values, you could be very tempted to write your Price descriptor like this:

```
class Price(object):
    def __init__(self):
        self.__price = 0

    def __get__(self, instance, owner):
        return self.__price

    def __set__(self, instance, value):
        if value < 0 or value > 100:
            raise         ValueError("Price
should be between 0 and 100.")
        self.__price = value

    def __delete__(self, instance):
        del self.__price
```

However, once you begin to create multiple instance of Book, you are going to have a bit of a problem:

```
>>> b1 = Book("J K Rowling", "Harry
Potter and the Chamber of Secrets", 12)
>>> b1.price

>>> b2 = Book("John Grisham", "Gray
Mountain", 13)
>>> b1.price
```

They key is in understanding that there can only a single instance of Price for the Book class so, whenever the descriptor value is changed, it will change the value of all instances. That behavior is incredibly useful for when you want to create some managed class attributes but it isn't what we want for this. To store separate values that are instance-specific, you will need to use `WeakRefDictionary`.

Using the Property Built-In Function

There is another way to build a descriptor and that is with the property built-in function. This is the signature for the function:

```
property(fget=None,        fset=None,
fdel=None, doc=None)
```

- `fget` – a method to get an attribute
- `fset` – a method to set an attribute
- `fdel` – a method to delete an attribute
- `doc` is a docstring

So, rather than defining one class-level descriptor for the purpose of managing the instance-specific values, property built-in function works by joining the instance methods of the class. The following is a very simple example – we have a Publisher class from the Inventory system and it has a managed name property. Every method that is passed into Properly will have a print statement that shows when the method is called:

```python
class Publisher(object):
    def __init__(self, name):
        self.__name = name

    def get_name(self):
        print("getting name")
        return self.__name

    def set_name(self, value):
        print("setting name")
        self.__name = value

    def delete_name(self):
        print("deleting name")
        del self.__name

    name = property(get_name, set_name,
delete_name, "Publisher name")
```

We want to access the name attribute so create a Publisher instance; this example show you the right methods that are being called:

```python
>>> p = Publisher("Random House")
>>> p.name
getting name
'Random House'
>>> p.name = "Wolters Kluwer"
setting name
>>> del p.name
deleting name
```

That is all for a basic look at descriptors. If you want a real challenge, look at what you have learned here and attempt to again implement the `@property` decorator – see how you get on.

Chapter 8:
Metaprogramming

Now that you are fully aware that a Python class is an object we can turn to something called metaprogramming. You are already well used to creating functions with the purpose of returning objects so it is unfair to consider these functions as object factories. They take an argument or two, create an object and then they return it. Look at the following example of a function that will create an object called int:

```
In [11]:
def int_factory(s):
    i = int(s)
    return i

i = int_factory('100')
print(i)
100
```

This is a very simple example but every function that you write in any normal program is going to be something along these lines - take your arguments, do a few things (operations) on them and then create your object and return it. However, keeping all of this in mind, there is absolutely nothing to stop you from creating an object that has a type of type (a class, in other words) and then returning it – we call this a metafunction:

```
In [12]:
def class_factory():
    class Foo(object):
```

```
        pass
    return Foo

F = class_factory()
f = F()
print(type(f))
<class '__main__.Foo'>
```

We already know that the `int_factory` function will construct an `int` instance and return it. In the same way, the `class_factory` function will construct an instance of type (a class) and returns it.

However, you may have noticed the slightly awkward construction. If you wanted to do some logic that was perhaps a little more complicated when you construct Foo, you would want, if you could, to avoid the nested indentations and to perhaps give the class a more dynamic definition. We can do this in a fairly easy way – we instantiate Foo directly from type, as in this example:

```
In [13]:
def class_factory():
    return type('Foo', (), {})

F = class_factory()
f = F()
print(type(f))
<class '__main__.Foo'>

In fact, the construct
In [14]:
```

```
class MyClass(object):
    pass
is exactly the same as the construct
In [15]:
MyClass = type('MyClass', (), {})
```

You should already know by now that `MyClass` is an instance of the type called `type`. We can see that explicitly in version 2 of the definition. There is one confusion that can potentially arise and that is from the way type is more commonly used – as a function that determines an object type. You should work at keeping these two keyword uses separate in your mind; in metafunctions, type is actually a class or a metaclass and `MyClass` is an instance of the type or class.

Let's look at what the type constructor arguments are:

```
type(name, bases, dct)
```

- `name` – this is a string that provides the name of the class that is being constructed
- `bases` – this is a tuple that provides the parent classes of the class under construction
- `dct` – this is a dictionary that provides the methods and the attributes of the class that is being constructed

An example – these two codes will have exactly the same results:

Example 1:

```
In [16]:
class Foo(object):
    i = 4

class Bar(Foo):
    def get_i(self):
        return self.i

b = Bar()
print(b.get_i())
4
```

Example 2:

```
In [17]:
Foo = type('Foo', (), dict(i=4))

Bar = type('Bar', (Foo,), dict(get_i =
lambda self: self.i))

b = Bar()
print(b.get_i())
4
```

Although this may seem to you to be a little bit too complicated, it is a very powerful way of creating classes dynamically as you need them,

Custom Metaclasses

Now let's make things a little more interesting. In the same way that you can extend and inherit from a class that you have created; you can also extend and inherit from the type metaclass. You can also create custom behaviors in your metaclass.

Example 1: Attribute Modification

Let's look at a simple example. We are going to create an API and in this API, the user will be able to create a whole set of interfaces which will have a file object in. Every interface must have its own string ID and it must be unique to that interface and each interface will also have its open file object. The user will then have the ability to write specialized methods that will allow them to accomplish specific tasks. There are some good ways of doing this without having to go into metaclasses but this example should hopefully show you clearly what is happening.

First, we are going to create the interface metaclass and it will be derived from type:

```
In [18]:
class InterfaceMeta(type):
    def __new__(cls, name, parents, dct):
        # create a class_id if it has
not been specified
        if 'class_id' not in dct:
```

```
        dct['class_id']              =
name.lower()

        # open that specified file so it
can be written to
        if 'file' in dct:
            filename = dct['file']
            dct['file'] = open(filename,
'w')

        # we must now call type.__new__
to finish off the initialization
        return          super(InterfaceMeta,
cls).__new__(cls, name, parents, dct)
```

Did you spot the modification to the input dictionary (the methods and attributes of your class)? We modified it so that it would add in a class ID if there want one already present and so that the filename would be replaced with a file object that points to the name.

Next, we will use our newly created interface metaclass for the construction and instantiation of a new interface object:

```
In [19]:
Interface    =    InterfaceMeta('Interface',
(), dict(file='tmp.txt'))

print(Interface.class_id)
print(Interface.file)
interface
<open  file  'tmp.txt',  mode  'w'  at
0x21b8810>
```

The behavior of this is exactly as we expect it to be – we have created a `class_id` variable and we have replaced the file class variable with the open file object. However, notice that the interface class creation, using the `InterfaceMeta`, is still a little bit awkward and it isn't that easy to read. This is where `__metaclass__` saves the day. We can do exactly the same thing by defining Interface in a different way:

```
In [20]:
class Interface(object):
    __metaclass__ = InterfaceMeta
    file = 'tmp.txt'

print(Interface.class_id)
print(Interface.file)
interface
<open file 'tmp.txt', mode 'w' at
0x21b8ae0>
```

When we define the `__metaclass__` attribute, we have informed the class that it shouldn't use type to construct the class; we should use `InterfaceMeta` instead. Let's make this a little more definite – note that the Interface type has now been reclassified as `InterfaceMeta`:

```
In [21]:
type(Interface)
Out[21]:
__main__.InterfaceMeta
```

Not only that, any class that is now derived from Interface is going to be constructed from the same metaclass:

```
In [22]:
class UserInterface(Interface):
    file = 'foo.txt'

print(UserInterface.file)
print(UserInterface.class_id)
<open    file    'foo.txt',    mode    'w'    at
0x21b8c00>
userinterface
```

This is a simple way of showing you that metaclasses can be used as way of creating very flexible and incredibly powerful project APIs. An example of that is Django project – this uses these kinds of constructions so that we can use concise declarations of powerful extensions to basic classes.

Example 2: Subclass Registration

There is another way to use metaclasses and that is to register all of the subclasses that are derived from a specific base class automatically. For example, you might have a basic database interface and want the user to have the ability to define interfaces which would then be stored automatically in a master registry. You could go about it this way:

```
In [23]:
class DBInterfaceMeta(type):
    # we will use __init__ instead of
__new__ here because we want
    # to be able to modify attributes of
this class *after* they have been
    # created
    def __init__(cls, name, bases, dct):
        if not hasattr(cls, 'registry'):
            # this is a base class.
Create an empty registry
            cls.registry = {}
        else:
            # this is the derived class.
Add cls to the registry
            interface_id = name.lower()
            cls.registry[interface_id]  =
cls

        super(DBInterfaceMeta,
cls).__init__(name, bases, dct)
```

The metaclass is doing a very simple thing here – it is adding a registry dictionary if there isn't already one present. It also adds the newly created class to the registry if that registry is already present. Let's look a bit closer at how this is going to work:

```
In [24]:
class DBInterface(object):
    __metaclass__ = DBInterfaceMeta

print(DBInterface.registry)
{}
```

It's time to create a few subclasses and then make sure that they have been added to the registry:

```
In [25]:
class FirstInterface(DBInterface):
    pass

class SecondInterface(DBInterface):
    pass

class
SecondInterfaceModified(SecondInterface):
    pass

print(DBInterface.registry)
{'firstinterface':                    <class
'__main__.FirstInterface'>,
'secondinterface':                   <class
'__main__.SecondInterface'>,
'secondinterfacemodified':           <class
'__main__.SecondInterfaceModified'>}
```

It works exactly as it should have done. You can use this together with any function that takes implementations from a registry and any of the user-defined objects that are Interface-derived will automatically be accounted for without the user having to register the new types manually.

When Metaclasses Should Be Used

We've looked at a few examples of metaclasses and a few ways in which they can be used in the creation of APIs. Although the metaclass is always working tirelessly away in the background in Python, you rarely have to consider them. The question is though, when do you need to start thinking about using a custom metaclass in a project. This isn't the easiest of questions to answer but this quote may just shed a little light on it for you:

"Metaclasses are deeper magic than 99% of users should ever worry about. If you wonder whether you need them, you don't (the people who actually need them know with certainty that they need them, and don't need an explanation about why)."
– Tim Peters

Chapter 9:
An Overview of Python Scripting Blender

Python is an interactive, interpreted OOP (Object Oriented Programming) language, featuring exceptions, modules, dynamic typing, classes and dynamic, very high-level data types. In short, it combines incredibly clear syntax with incredible power.

Blender is an open-source powerful modeling platform packed full of features that rival any of the professional packages, like Maya and 3D Studio Max. As well as having a full set of modeling tools, Blender is also home to a strong Python API and this allows you to create add-ons and scripts. Best of all, Blender is free.

Python scripts are a very versatile and powerful way of extending the functionality of Blender to the extent that most Blender areas can be scripted, including Import and Export, Animation, Object Creation, Rendering and repetitive task scripting.

Blender works by letting you change the viewport layout to reflect many different ways to work. For example, you might want a set of windows for rendering and then a different set for modeling and the same can be said of scripting Blender features a preset layout for scripting that can be customized as per your requirements.

The Blender interface includes:

- A Text Editor
- A Python Console
- An Info Window
- A Blender Console
- An Interface Elements

Text Editor

This is a standard editor that allows you to edit, load and save your Python script files. You can do all the standard stuff like highlighting syntax and line numbering but there is no option for code completion

Python Console

Combined with the text editor, the Python console provides a very handy way of exploring the Python API in a more efficient way whilst you are coding. The Python console also offers a good Autocomplete feature which lets you explore through the Python API

Info Window

The Info window or viewport in Blender lets you see all the most recent activity in Blender as executable commands. This is a great feature for when you want to prototype a process through the use of modeling methods and then put them into a script.

Blender Console

Blender also features a console window which, in all honesty, is no different to your operating system command prompt. It is useful for printing values when you are testing code.

Bonus Chapter: Django Web Development with Python

Django is a Python web framework that allows for quick development of websites that are secure and easy to maintain. Django was built be very experienced developers to take care of most of the hassle that surrounds web development, leaving you free to write your app without having to go through all the hoops to do it.

Django was first developed between 2003 and 2005 by a team of web developers who started out creating and maintaining a bunch of newspaper websites. Once they had created a few, they started to factor out some of the more common design patterns and code and reuse it. This grew into a generic framework for web development and, in 2005 it was open-sourced as Django.

Over time, Django has grown and it has improved, from its very first release in 2008 right up to the most recent version. Each release has brought bug fixes and new functions, from support for new database types, caching and template engines, right through to generic classes and view functions – this help to cut down on the code that has to be written for several different programming tasks.

As a result, Django is a thriving open-source project, complete with thousands of contributors and users. While there are still some of the original features left, Django has grown into one of the most versatile web development frameworks that ever existed.

With Django, you can write software that is:

Complete

Think of every toy or game that you have ever bought that has the batteries included, so that you can use it straight out of the box. That is Django; it provides just about everything that you might want to do from the off and, because everything is part of the same thing, it all works together seamlessly, follows the same consistent principles of design and it includes the most up to date and extensive documentation.

Versatile

If you can think of a website type, you can almost certainly use Django to build it. It has been used to build Wikis, content management systems, news websites and social networking sites. It works with any client-side framework and it is able to deliver content in just about any format, and that includes RSS feeds, HTML, XML, JSON, etc.

Internally, Django provides you with choices for pretty much any functionality you could want and it can be extended to take in other components as required.

Secure

Django can also help you to avoid many of the more common security errors that are made by providing you with a framework fully engineered to do all the right stuff in giving your website automatic protection. For example, it can give you a highly secure way of managing user accounts, managing passwords, avoiding simple but common errors like using cookies to store session information – this makes that information highly vulnerable; a cookie merely stores a key while the data should be stored in a database. It also helps you avoid storing passwords instead of the password hash.

For those that don't know, a password hash is a value of fixed length that is created when a password is sent through a cryptographic hash function. Django is able to see if the password that has been entered is the right one by putting it through the hash function and checking the output against the hash value in storage.

Django also provides protection by default against a wide range of known vulnerabilities, such as cross-site scripting, SQL injection, clickjacking and cross-site request forgery.

Scalable

The component-based architecture that Django uses dictates that each bit of the architecture is completely independent of all the other bits; that means they can be changed or replaced as needed. By having this type of separation, increased traffic can be scaled for through the addition of hardware at any level, such as database servers, caching servers and application servers.

Maintainable

Design patterns and principles that encourage reusable and maintainable code is what is used in Django. It makes good use of the DRY principle – Don't Repeat Yourself – meaning there is no duplication that is not necessary and this, in turn, cuts the amount of code needed. Django promotes grouping of functionality that is related into applications that are reusable and also groups code that is related into modules.

Portable

Django is based in Python and this makes it possible that it runs on several different platforms. This means that you are not stuck with using just one specified platform and your applications will run on all the different implementations of Mac, Windows, and Linux. As well as that, Django is thoroughly supported by several different web hosting providers and these will provide you with the right infrastructure and the right documentation for hosting a Django website.

What Django Code Looks Like

In a traditional website, one that is data-driven, the web applications will wait for the HTTP requests to come from the client, such as a web browser. When that request has been received, the application will use the URL and some information from both GET and POST data to work out what is needed. Depending on the requirements, information may then be read or written from a database or another task may be performed. The application then returns the response to the browser and it will often insert the data it has retrieved into a placeholder within an HTML template to create an HTML page.

In a Django web application, the code that is responsible for handling each of the following steps into their own files:

- **URL** – while requests from each and every URL can be processed through one function, it is better and easier to maintain if a separate view function is written to for each resource. In order for the HTTP requests to be directed to the right view, based on the URL, a URL mapper is used. This is also able to match digit or string patterns that show up in a URL and pass them as data to a view function.

- **View** – this is a request handler function and it will receive an HTTP request and return it as an HTTP response. The views will access the data that is needed to satisfy a request through models and it will delegate response formatting to templates

- **Model** – a model is a Python object that is used to define the structure of the data in an application It also provides the mechanisms needed to add, modify and delete as well as querying database records.

- **Template** – this is a text file that is used to define the layout or the structure of a file, like an HTML page, using placeholders as a representation of the content. Views will create HTML pages dynamically through the use of an HTML template and will populate it with data that comes from a model. The template is a method of defining structure in any file type, not just HTML

Conclusion

Thank you again for downloading this book!

I hope this book was able to help you to improve and further your knowledge on Python computer programming.

The next step is to practice, that's all. Computer programming concepts change regularly; old ones disappear or are updated and new ones appear and, if you don't keep up with it, you will lose it. You have come so far; the last thing you want to do is have to start again.

There are plenty of resources for you to choose from on the internet; books, forums, and courses, all of which will help you go further in your quest to become a top Python programmer.

Finally, if you enjoyed this book, then I'd like to ask you for a favor, would you be kind enough to leave a review for this book on Amazon? It'd be greatly appreciated!

Thank you and good luck!

JavaScript:

Advanced Guide to Programming Code

with JavaScript

Charlie Masterson

Introduction

I want to thank you and congratulate you for owning my book, *"JavaScript: Advanced Guide to Programming Code with JavaScript"*.

This book contains a whole set of proven steps and strategies to help you learn more advanced JavaScript code. I must stress the word "Advanced" here – this book is not for you if you have not learnt the basics of JavaScript; it is aimed at those with prior knowledge and experience who want to further their knowledge and become better JavaScript programmers.

You can go a long way in JavaScript just by using the basics but if you want to make the most of the power that JavaScript has to offer you need to learn a few more advanced concepts and techniques. These are designed to help you write code that is more expressive and can be reused. These are patterns that define a few features that you might not find in other computer programming languages and that is what makes this such a unique and powerful language.

If this is your first computer programming language, you will more than likely find some of the patterns a little on the strange side but, with the explanations and the examples I have included, as well as me exercises for you to do (With the answers!), you will soon become familiar with it. You will find some of the chapters in this book are quite short while others are somewhat longer. I have tried to keep everything as concise as possible to make it easier for you to take it all in. You won't find any long introductions in each chapter either; you should be at a level now where I can jump straight in and explain as I go along!

Thank you again for reading my book; I truly hope that you find it useful and I wish you luck as you work your way through these advanced JavaScript techniques.

Chapter 1: Optional Function Arguments

When a function is declared in JavaScript, the function expects would usually have an argument list in it:

Example:

CODE:

```
    function    sumValues(val1,    val2,
val3) {

            return val1 + val2 + val3;

    }
```

Unfortunately, this won't guarantee that your function is going to be called, every time, with three arguments. It is OK for the function to be passed with less or more than three:

Example:

```
var result1 = sumValues(3, 5, 6, 2, 7);

var result2 = sumValues(12, 20);
```

Both of these calls are going to result in some very surprising results from the perspective of the caller.

In the first example, as we are only expecting three arguments, 2 and 7, which are the extra values, are going to be ignored. This isn't good because the value that is returned won't be what was expected by the calling code.

The second example really isn't any better; in fact, it's worse. In this example, we only passed two arguments so what happened to val3? The value of val3 will be undefined and the result of this is the sum of NaN which really isn't what we wanted so we need to fix this so that this type of situation can be avoided in the future:

Example:

```
function    sumValues(val1,    val2,
val3) {

    if (val1 === undefined) {

        val1 = 0;

    }


    if (val2 === undefined) {

        val2 = 0;

    }


    if (val3 === undefined) {

        val3 = 0;

    }


    return val1 + val2 + val3;

}
```

```
    var result1 = sumValues(3, 5, 6, 2,
7);

    var result2 = sumValues(12, 20);


    alert(result1);

    alert(result2);
```

If you were to run that again now, you would see that the second function call now no longer results in NaN. Instead, we get the result of 32, most likely what was expected by the calling code.

Now we have a function that will add three numbers but there is still something missing; it isn't quite right or very useful. At some time, you are going to want to add more numbers and you really don't want to have to update your code each time so it will accept additional parameters. Fortunately, JavaScript has the answer.

Each function, when it is called, will have a variable that is called arguments. This variable is an array containing every argument that has been passed to the function. So, let's go back to that example; when you call sumValues for the first time, the array will have [3, 5, 6, 2, 7] and the second time it will have [12, 20].

What we mean by this is that the passed parameters can be ignored and we can concentrate on dealing with the arguments array only. An update to the function would look like this:

Example:

```
function sumValues() {

    var sum = 0;

        for (var i = 0; i <
arguments.length; i++) {

            sum += arguments[i];

        }

        return sum;

    }


    var result1 = sumValues(3, 5, 6, 2,
7);

    var result2 = sumValues(12, 20);


    alert(result1);

    alert(result2);
```

Did you spot that we removed the parameter list? Now the values come straight from the array and, when the example is run again, the returned values are right and are exactly what the calling code expected.

What we have now is a full function that will accept any number of parameters that you throw at it and it will always return the value as the sum of all arguments.

Chapter 2:
Truthy and Falsy

As you already know, JavaScript contains a Boolean data type. This data type only has two values – true or false. Boolean expressions, for example, a == b, will also evaluate to Boolean values but that isn't all you need to know.

When you use a non-Boolean expression in a Boolean context, for example, an if condition, those expressions will implicitly convert to Booleans, in a process called type coercion. For example, if you have the expression `if (1) {alert('Hi')}`,1 would be interpreted as true, meaning that the alert will appear. Value 1 is known as truthy while value 0 is falsy.

When we use that in a context that is expecting a Boolean value, you can use any JavaScript expression:

Example:

```
var truthies = [

      "false",

      "0",

      -1,

      "null",

      "undefined",

      "NaN",

      5/0,

      Infinity
```

```javascript
];

var foo;

var falsies = [

    null,

    undefined,

    foo,

    0,

    NaN,

    ""

];



    for (var t=0; t<truthies.length;
t++) {

        document.write("<li>"        +
truthies[t]      +     "    :    "     +
Boolean(truthies[t]) + "</li>");

    }



    for (var f=0; f<falsies.length;
f++) {

        document.write("<li>"          +
falsies[f] + " : " + Boolean(falsies[f])
+ "</li>");
```

}

Go to a browser and open that page above; what do you see? You will notice ow all the different values are evaluated when they are implicitly converted into Booleans.

Below is a list of how the different values will be converted:

Value   Truthy or Falsy Explanation

0   falsy
0 is always falsy

"0"   truthy
all non-sera strings are always truthy

-1   truthy
any number that is not 0 is truthy

null   falsy
null is always falsy

"null"   truthy
another non-zero string, therefore truthy

undefined   falsy
undefined is always falsy

"undefined"   truthy
non-zero string, truthy

NaN   falsy
NaN is always falsy

"NaN"   truthy
non-zero string

Infinity   truthy   a
reserved keyword and non-zero

5/0	truthy		
	evaluates to Infinity		

""(empty string)	falsy		Zero
strings are always falsy			

"false"	truthy		
	Non-zero string		

The reason we have the strictly or triple = (===) comparison operator is type coercion. ==, which is the regular equality operator, will apply type coercion and, on occasion, your comparisons will not give you the result that you expect. Have a look at this example:

Example:

```
var num = 0;

if (num == "") {

    alert('Hey, I did not expect to see this.');

}

if (num === "") {

    alert('This will not be displayed.');

}
```

We have compared two falsy values in conditional one and they will both be resolved, through type coercion, to false. This makes the comparison result as true, most likely not what the intent of this code was.

In order to detect the differences in type, i.e. between string and number, you would use the === operator, as you can see in the second if statement.

Type Coercion

This is an exercise for you, it should take about 5 to 10 minutes to complete. You are going to debug a simple script and fix it:

- In your editor, open this page: AdvancedTechniques/Exercises/type-coercion.html
- Work out what is wrong with the code
- Make the required fixes
- Test your solution in your browser

Solution:

This is what you should have got:

```
var answer = prompt("What is 10-10?","");

if (answer === "0") {

    alert("Right!");

} else {

    alert("Wrong!");

}
```

You probably found that a bit harder than you thought it would be, In the original code, if the user were to press on OK on their prompt without inputting anything, the alert would be "Right!". This is because it is an empty string – remember, empty strings and 0 are both falsy.

So what do you need to do? Initial thoughts might be that you just change == to === as a way of differentiating between types but if you were to do that and test it, the alert will always read "Wrong!" even if you used 0.

The problem here is that the value in the prompt is actually a string and string "0" doesn't strictly equal to number 0. The answer is to change the condition so that it says `answer==="0"`.

Chapter 3: Default Operators

&& and || are Boolean operators that use truthy and falsy to resolve the operands to Boolean values. If you have used other programming languages, you will probably be thinking that Boolean operator results are always true or false. In JavaScript, that isn't strictly true.

With the JavaScript language, Boolean operation results are always the value of the particular operand that was the determining factor in the operation result. Let me make that a little clearer:

Example:

```
var a = 0, b = NaN, c = 1, d = "hi";

var result = ( a || b || c || d );

alert("Result: " + result);


result = ( d && c && b && a );

alert("Result: " + result);
```

(a || b || c || d) is the first Boolean expression and it will be evaluated left to right until it reaches a conclusion. || is a Boolean OR operator and this only requires that one operand is a truthy for the entire result to be true. In the case of the example above:

- a = 0 and zero is always falsy. The valuation will continue with the rest of the operands because falsy isn't yet determining anything. Only one truthy value is required for the entire statement to be true
- b is Nan, which is also falsy. The same situation occurs and we must continue to evaluate
- c is 1 and this is truthy. From here on, we have no need to evaluate any more operands because the expression is going to result in true.

There is a catch though – have you worked it out? Instead of a strictly true result, we will get a truthy value that stopped the evaluation, in the case of this example, c. the displayed message will read "Result: 1"

You may already expect that the And operator, && works in pretty much the same way but using opposite conditions. This operator will return the value of the last operand that was evaluated and that will be either the first falsy or, where all the operands are truthy, the final one in the expression. Let's say that we follow the sequence for the expression (d && c && b && a) that we did in the case of the OR operator. You will see that both d and c are truthy so you must keep on going; when you get to b, a falsy, the evaluation will halt and the return will be b with the displayed message reading "Result: NaN".

You might be sitting there thinking, what use is any of this? The behavior you have seen here, the return of the first value that is conclusive, is a very handy behavior to ensure the initialization of a variable.

Look at the example of a function below:

```
function checkLength(text, min, max){

    min = min || 1;

    max = max || 10000;


    if    (text.length    <    min    ||
text.length > max) {

        return false;

    }

    return true;

}
```

In line one and two of the example, we have made sure that a valid value is always assigned to min and max. Because of this, the function can be called like checkValue("abc"). The parameters for both the min and max will start with the value undefined.

When we get to `min = min || 1;` all we are doing is assigning a value of 1 to min, just to make sure that it will override undefined, In the same way, max is assigned a value of 10000.

Were we to have passed the real values for the parameters, as in the example `checkLength("abc", 2, 10)` these values would have been retained as they are truthy.

When we use the || operator, we are, in effect giving default values to the parameters and that is why we call the operator the default operator, at least in this context. The operator is used to replace longer code like:

```
if (min === undefined) {

        min = 1;

}
```

To become:

```
min = min || 1;
```

Have a look at another example of how to use the default operator to shorten your code. This code

```
var contactInfo;

if (email) {

        contactInfo = email;
```

```
} else if (phone) {

    contactInfo = phone;

} else if (streetAddress) {

    contactInfo = streetAddress;

}
```

Can be significantly shortened to:

```
var contactInfo = email || phone ||
streetAddress;
```

Note: do be careful when you use this operator with a variable that accepts falsy values. Look at this code example to see where the danger lies:

Example:

```
function calculatePrice(basePrice, tax) {

    basePrice = basePrice || 0;

    tax = tax || .1; //default tax is
10%

    var price = (basePrice * (1 +
tax)).toFixed(2);

    alert("The price including tax is "
+ price);

}


calculatePrice(100, 0); //no tax
```

The function `calculatePrice()` is using the default operator as a way setting a default tax of 1. The problem arises when 0 is passed as the tax value. Your intent with the code is an indication of no tax but, as 0 is falsy, `tax = tax || .1` will evaluate to .1.

This can be fixed by changing `tax = tax || .1` to `tax = (tax === 0) ? 0 : tax || .1;`.

Applying Defaults to Function Parameters

This exercise should take you about 5 to 15 minutes to complete. We are going to go back to an example we used earlier and use || as a way of handling optional parameters.

- Open
  AdvancedTechniques/Exercises/sumAll
  -defaults.html in your editor
- Edit the sumValues() to make use of the
  || operator instead of using if blocks

Example:

```
<!DOCTYPE HTML>

<html>

<head>

<meta charset="UTF-8">
```

```html
<title>Sum all numbers, default operator</title>

<script type="text/javascript">

    function sumValues(val1, val2, val3) {

        if (val1 === undefined) {

            val1 = 0;

        }


        if (val2 === undefined) {

            val2 = 0;

        }


        if (val3 === undefined) {

            val3 = 0;

        }


        return val1 + val2 + val3;

    }


    var result1 = sumValues(3, 5, 6, 2, 7);

    var result2 = sumValues(12, 20);
```

```
        alert(result1);

        alert(result2);

</script>

</head>

<body>

<p>Nothing to show here.</p>

</body>

</html>
```

The Solution:

```
<!DOCTYPE HTML>

<html>

<head>

<meta charset="UTF-8">

<title>Sum     all     numbers,     default
operator</title>

<script type="text/javascript">

        function    sumValues(val1,     val2,
val3) {

            val1 = val1 || 0;

            val2 = val2 || 0;

            val3 = val3 || 0;
```

```
            return val1 + val2 + val3;

    }


    var result1 = sumValues(3, 5, 6, 2,
7);

    var result2 = sumValues(12, 20);


    alert(result1);

    alert(result2);
</script>

</head>

<body>

<p>Nothing to show here.</p>

</body>

</html>
```

Chapter 4:
Functions Passed
as Arguments

Functions in JavaScript are first-class objects, not just a block of immutable code that is only able to be invoked. Instead, every function that is declared then becomes an object, complete with its own methods and properties, and these can be passed in the same way as any object can.

Have a look at the following example to see how a function can be used as a parameter to another function:

Example:

```
//let's make an array that contains
5 values

var values = [5, 2, 11, -7, 1];


//this function will add the values
of 'a' and 'b' and will return the sum

function add(a, b) {

    return a+b;

}


//this function will multiply the
value of 'a' times 'b' and will return
the result

function multiply(a, b) {

    return a*b;
```

```
        }


        /* the 1st param passed is the
numbers (in this case, the array of
values)

        * the 2nd param passed is the
initial Value (could be 0, 1, or
whatever)

        * the 3rd param passed is the
operation - which will be one of the
functions that is declared above (add or
subtract)

        */

        function          combineAll(nums,
initialValue, operation) {

        //let's initialize the local
variable 'runningResult' with the
initialValue passed to it

        var      runningResult      =
initialValue;

        //loop the nums array

        for   (var   i=0;   i   <
nums.length; i++) {

            /* for each iteration,
call the function (which can be add or
multiply) passing the 2 params

            * on   the   first
iteration,   runningResult   is   the
```

```
initialValue; after that, value returned
from operation(runningResult, nums[i])

                * nums[i] refers to
the current number in the iteration; the
1st is 5, then 2, and so on.

                */

                runningResult        =
operation(runningResult, nums[i]);

        }

        return runningResult;

    }


    //notice the 3rd param passes the
"add" function - you can pass a function
into another function!

        var sum = combineAll(values, 0,
add);


    //notice the 3rd param passes the
"multiply" function - you can pass a
function into another function!

        var product = combineAll(values, 1,
multiply);


        alert("Sum: " + sum); //should be
12: 5+2+11+(-7)+1
```

```
    alert("Product:   "   +    product);
//should be -770: 5x2x11x-7x1
```

You might be wondering what this function means - `var sum = combineAll(values, 0, add);`. In the above example, the function add is being passed as parameter three of `combineAll`. At this moment, we are not going to invoke add, merely pass a reference. Did you spot that the parentheses were not used after add? That should be a little tip that we are not invoking any function.

The code line that will invoke add reads:

```
runningResult  =  operation(runningResult,
nums[i]);
```

A reference to add the operation parameter was received by this and, when the operation is invoked, you will see that add is being called and it returns the value of both of the sums that were passed to it.

This is a vital technique and we often call the `combineAll` function to reduce. Take some time to look over the code and run it until you are comfortable with it. We are going to be using this in the following chapters so you need to understand it.

Anonymous Functions

Looking back at the example we used before, the add and multiply functions were only referred to on one occasion, in the call to combineAll. If you were to stick with that pattern, you would need to make a new function for every new combination desire that you wanted, for example, concatenation, just so you could pass it to combineAll. Doesn't that seem like rather a complicated way of doing something that is actually quite simple?

You will be pleased to learn that you don't have to declare each function. In fact, you don't even need to come up with any names for them. In JavaScript, we can create functions on the fly, whenever you need one that is only going to be used in that one location. Even better, the syntax used is quite simple:

```
function (arg1, arg2) {

    //function statements here

    }
```

Because these functions are not named, we call them anonymous functions.

Let's go back to a previous example and use these anonymous functions to take the place of the single-use functions:

Example:

```
var values = [5, 2, 11, -7, 1];
```

```javascript
function                  combineAll(nums,
initialValue, operation) {

        var        runningResult      =
initialValue;

        for     (var    i=0;    i    <
nums.length; i++) {

            runningResult          =
operation(runningResult, nums[i]);

        }

        return runningResult;

    }


    var  sum  =   combineAll(values,  0,
function (a, b) {

            return a+b;

        });


    var product = combineAll(values, 1,
function (a, b) {

            return a*b;

        });


    var  list  =  combineAll(values,  1,
function (a, b) {

            return a + ", " + b;
```

```
        });
```

```
    alert("Sum: " + sum);

    alert("Product: " + product);

    alert("Number List: " + list);
```

There are three anonymous functions in here; the first and second ones replace where the add and multiply functions used to be defined and the third is used as a way of concatenating integers into a list, each separated by a comma.

Chapter 5:
Nested Functions

As JavaScript functions are another type of JavaScript object, we are able to make a function that is inside another function. We call these nested functions, sometimes known as inner functions. Have a look at the example that shows you how to create one function and then use it inside another function:

Example:

```
var values = [5, 2, 11, -7, 1];


function            combineAll(nums,
initialValue, operator) {

    var     runningResult    =
initialValue;

        for    (var    i=0;    i    <
nums.length; i++) {

            runningResult        =
calculate(nums[i]);

        }

    return runningResult;


    function calculate(num) {
        switch
(operator.toLowerCase()) {

            case "+" :
```

```javascript
                        return
runningResult + num;

                    case "x" :

                        return
runningResult * num;

                    case "*" :

                        return
runningResult * num;

                    case "a" :

                        return
runningResult + ", " + num;

                }

            }

        }


    var  sum  =  combineAll(values,  0,
"+");

    var product = combineAll(values, 1,
"x");

    var  list  =  combineAll(values,  1,
"a");


    alert("Sum: " + sum);

    alert("Product: " + product);

    alert("Number List: " + list);
```

You are going to see more of these but, for now, take note of the way in which `calculate()` accesses both operator and `runningResult,` both of which have been scoped to the function, `combineAll().`

Chapter 6:
Variable Scope

JavaScript variables are declared with the use of the var keyword and they will be either locally or globally scoped. To be globally scoped, a variable must meet any of the following conditions:

- The variable has been declared outside a function
- The variable has been used without the use of the var keyword to declare it

To be locally scoped, a variable has to be declared in another function with the var keyword.

Global variables can be accessed from anywhere in the JavaScript code:

Example:

```
var maxNum; //global

function prepare() {

        var maxNum = 5; //local to
function

        //let's forget the "var" in
the "for" declaration

        for (i=0; i <= maxNum; ++i) {
//no var, so i will be global

                //do something

        }

}
```

```
prepare();

alert(maxNum); //undefined

alert(i);    //6    (because    it    is
globally scoped)
```

Note that maxNum is a globally declared variable but has not got a value assigned to it. It has been declared inside the prepare() function and has been given a value of 5.

Have a look at the maxNum value after prepare(), has been called. The value has been left as undefined. The reason for this is because the global variable is being rea and we can't have access to the function variable from the outside of the function.

We can, however, access variable i, simply because we gave it a value inside the function without using var to declare it.

Because there is no block scope within JavaScript, variables will never be local to a for loop or an if statement.

Chapter 7:
Observing and
Capturing Events

Most likely you are more used to using HTML event handlers, such as "on" attributes, as a way of capturing events – see the example below:

Example:

```
<ul>

    <li
onclick="document.bgColor='red';">Red</li
>

    <li
onclick="document.bgColor='orange';">Oran
ge</li>

    <li
onclick="document.bgColor='green';">Green
</li>

    <li
onclick="document.bgColor='blue';">Blue</
li>

</ul>
```

However, it is far better to keep HTML and JavaScript separate from one another.

The eval() Function

Why are we talking about this function here? It is to simply acknowledge that it exists and to tell you NOT to use it. I will tell you why but first you need to know what it does.

eval is used to compile a string and execute it, the string will contain JavaScript code and it can be something very simple, an expression like "2 + 3" or it can be a longer more complex script, with all sorts of functions and other things in it.

Look at the following example: this is similar to what you might find on the internet in live web sites:

Example:

```
    function     getProperty(objectName,
propertyName) {

        //expression     will      be:
document.title

        var expression = objectName +
"." + propertyName;

        console.log(expression);

        //the    eval()    function    will
evaluate      the       expression,      so
document.title gives us the title of the
document

        var        propertyValue       =
eval(expression);

        return propertyValue;

    }
```

```
      var prop = "title"; //assume that
this was given by the user

      alert(getProperty("document",
prop));
```

This function will come up with an expression by taking an object name and concatenating it with a dot and the name of a property. It then evaluates the expression using `eval()`. While it is an incredibly powerful function, it also has the potential to be very dangerous and is not terribly efficient. Why is it dangerous? Because it usually used as way of evaluating input from a user and this isn't always the safest thing to do. The inefficiency side comes from the fact that every call to `eval()` will start a JavaScript compiler.

Using the function normally indicates a real lack of knowledge on the part of the developer. In the above example, we could have gone down the route of using the [] property accessor. We would have got the same from alert(window[prop]); without the need to start the compiler just to get the value of the property.

Remember: avoid using eval as much as you possibly can because it will only cause problems in your code.

Chapter 8:
Error Handling

It doesn't matter how carefully you write your code, errors will always appear. Mostly, they will be runtime errors that arise from things you can't predict. Other times, they are bugs or your code not behaving as it is supposed to. Fortunately, JavaScript provides you with the tools you need to deal with both types of error and that is what we are going to talk about in this chapter.

Runtime Errors

Web browsers can be incredibly hostile places and it is pretty much guaranteed that you will be forever dealing with runtime errors. Users put in wrong inputs in ways you truly didn't think was possible. A new version of the browser can change the way things work and Ajax calls could fail for many different reasons.

Much of the time, there is nothing you can do to stop a runtime error but there are ways to deal with them to make things a little less traumatic for the user.

Unhandled Errors:

Have a look at this example, it seems trivial:

Example:

```
function getInput() {

    var name = prompt('Type your
name');
```

```
        alert('Your    name    has    '    +
name.length + ' letters.');

}

getInput();
```

Look at the code properly; it might not be that obvious to begin with but this is a bug waiting to happen. If a user were to click or press ESC or Cancel, a null will be returned by the prompt() function and this will give the net line a null reference error and make it fail.

If the developer doesn't do anything about this, the end user will get a browser message that means absolutely nothing to them. Depending on how the user has configured their settings or browser, they may not get an on-screen message; it might show up as a small icon in the status bar, an icon which could be missed easily and leave users believing that the application is just not responding.

Globally Handed Errors:

There is an event known as on error in a window object and this might be invoked whenever an unhandled error shows up on the page. For example:

Example:

```javascript
window.onerror = function (message, url,
lineNo) {

    alert(

        'Error: ' + message +

        '\n Url: ' + url +

        '\n Line Number: ' + lineNo);

    return true;

}


function getInput() {

    var name = prompt('Type your
name');

    alert('Your name has ' +
name.length + ' letters.');

}

getInput();
```

As you can see from this example, the event passes three arguments to the function. The first is the error message, the second is the URL of the file that has the error in it, very useful if this is an external .js file, and the third shows the line number that the error is on in that specific file.

The return true is telling the browser that the developer has dealt with this; if false were returned, the browser would treat this as an unhandled error and the on-screen or status bar message would show up on the user's screen.

Structured Error Handling

As with anything, the very best way to deal with an error is to detect it as near to where it occurs as you can. This will make it easier for you to know what to do with it. JavaScript will use try...catch...finally block to implement structured error handling:

```
try {

    //try statements

} catch (error) {

    //catch statements

} finally {

    //finally statements

}
```

This is a very simple premise; if the error occurs in statements that are in the try block, the statements in the catch block are executed and the error is passed straight to the error variable. The finally block is an optional one and, if it used, it will always be executed last whether there is an error or not.

What can we do to make our code catch the error?

Example:

```javascript
window.onerror = function (message, url,
lineNo) {

    alert(

        'Error: ' + message +

        '\n Url: ' + url +

        '\n Line Number: ' + lineNo);

    return true;

}


function getInput() {

    try {

        var          name          =
window.prompt('Type your name');

        alert('Your   name   has   ' +
name.length + ' letters.');

    } catch (error) {

        alert('The   error   was:   ' +
error.name +

        '\n The error message was: '
+ error.message);

    } finally {

        //do cleanup

    }
```

```
}

getInput();
```

There are two important properties in the error object – message and name. Message has the error message that we already know about while name contains information about what type of error it was. We use this information to determine what to do about the error.

One piece of good advice for any programmer is to handle an error on the spot only if you are 100% certain you know what it is and that you know exactly how to fix it, rather than suppressing it. To target the handling code better, it can be changed just to handle errors that are called TypeError – this is the name of the error that has been identified for the bug:

Example:

```
window.onerror = function (message, url,
lineNo) {

    alert(

        'Error: ' + message +

        '\n Url: ' + url +

        '\n Line Number: ' + lineNo);

    return true;

}
```

```javascript
function getInput() {

    try {

        var              name              =
window.prompt('Type your name');

        alert('Your   name   has   '   +
name.length + ' letters.');

    } catch (error) {

        if         (error.name         ==
'TypeError') {

            alert('Please            try
again.');

            getInput();

        } else      {

            throw error;

        }

    } finally {

        //do cleanup

    }

}

getInput();
```

If a different error were to occur, not likely in
this simple example, it would not be handled.
The throw statement will send the error on just
as though we hadn't used try...catch...finally

block. The error will appear later on down the line.

Throwing Custom Errors

Th throw statement can be used to throw up custom errors and there is only one recommendation here – the error object must have name and message properties that are consistent with the built-in handling method. Look at this example:

```
throw {

    name: 'InvalidColorError',

    message: 'The given color is not a
valid color value.'

};
```

Chapter 9:
'delete' Operator

We use the 'delete' operator as way of deleting object properties and array elements. Be very clear on this – deleting is not the same as setting a value to null. Deleting removes the element or property, making it undefined, while setting as value as null will retain the element or object while setting it a value of null. Have a look at this example as an illustration:

Example:

```
<!DOCTYPE HTML>

<html>

<head>

<meta charset="UTF-8">

<script type="text/javascript">

    var colors = [];

    colors["red"] = "#f00";

    colors["green"] = "#060";

    colors["blue"] = "#00f";

    colors["yellow"] = "#ff0";

    colors["orange"] = "#0ff";


    function deleteItem() {

        delete colors["blue"];
```

```javascript
        showArray();

        revealArray();

    }


    function setToNull() {

        colors["blue"] = null;

        showArray();

        revealArray();

    }


    function showArray() {

            var          output          =
document.getElementById("colors");

            var strOutput = "<ol>";

            for (var i in colors) {

                    strOutput     +=     "<li
style='color:" + colors[i] + ";'>" + i +
"</li>";

            }

            strOutput += "</ol>";

            output.innerHTML=strOutput;

    }
```

```
function revealArray() {

        var       colorsCode       =
document.getElementById("colors-code");

        var strOutput = "&lt;ol&gt;";

        for (var i in colors) {

                strOutput+="\n\t&lt;li
style='color:" + colors[i] + ";'&gt;" + i
+ "&lt;/li&gt;";

        }

        strOutput += "\n&lt;/ol&gt;";


    colorsCode.innerHTML=strOutput;

    }

</script>

<title>Delete vs. Setting to NULL</title>

</head>

<body
onload="showArray();revealArray();">

<button              id="set-to-null"
onclick="setToNull();">Set     Blue     to
Null</button>

<button                    id="del"
onclick="deleteItem();">Delete
Blue</button>

<output id="colors"></output>

<pre id="colors-code"></pre>
```

```
</body>

</html>
```

Forget   about   the
functions `showArray()` and `revealArray()` for
now. Do note however that when the button for
Set Blue to Null is clicked, the array element
will stay put but will be an invalid color of null.
When Delete Blue button is clicked, the array
element will be deleted.

Regular Expressions

This is a quick introduction to the next few
chapters, where we go over regular
expressions. These are used for pattern
matching and this can be very helpful when it
comes to form validation. For example, you can
use a regular expression to check that an email
address that has been input into a form filed is
correct in terms of syntax. You can create
regular expressions in two ways in JavaScript:

Literal Syntax:

```
var reExample = /pattern/;
```

RegExp() Constructor

```
var reExample = new RegExp("pattern");
```

If you already know the pattern you are going
to use, there isn't any real difference between
these. However, if you don't know which patter

you are going to use, the easiest one is the `RegExp()` constructor.

Chapter 10: Regular Expressions – Methods

The JavaScript regular expression method contains two main methods for string testing: test() and exec().

The `exec()` Method

This method takes an argument and a string and checks to see if there are one or more matches in the string to a pattern that is specified in the regular expressions. If the matches are found, a result array is returned by the method showing the starting point of each match. If there are no matches, null is returned.

The `test()` Method

This method will also take a string and an argument and check the string for pattern matches. If there is a match, true will be returned; if not, false is returned. This is incredibly useful in form validations scripts.

The following example show how to use this to test a social security number. Ignore the regular expression syntax for now, we will be looking at that in the next chapter:

Example:

```
RegularExpressions/Demos/SsnChecker.html

<!DOCTYPE HTML>

<html>
```

```html
<head>

<meta charset="UTF-8">

<title>ssn Checker</title>

<script type="text/javascript">

var  reSSN  =  /^[0-9]{3}[\-  ]?[0-9]{2}[\-
]?[0-9]{4}$/;


function checkSsn(ssn){

     if (reSSN.test(ssn)) {

          alert("VALID SSN");

     } else {

          alert("INVALID SSN");

     }

}

</script>

</head>

<body>

     <form onsubmit="return false;">

          <input type="text" name="ssn"
size="20">

          <input           type="button"
value="Check"
```

```
        onclick="checkSsn(this.form.ssn.val
ue);">

        </form>

</body>

</html>
```

Let's take a closer look at the code.

First, we have declared a variable that contains a regular expression object relating to a social security number

Second, we have created a function called `checkSsn()`. This function takes an argument, ssn, which is also a string, and passes it to the regular expression to see if there is a match. For this, the `test()` method is used. If there is a match, the function will alert "VALID SSN". If there is no match, "INVALID SSN" is alerted instead.

Lastly, a form inserted in the page body provides a field for a user to input a social security number along with a button that will pass the number to the `checkSsn()` function.

Flags

If a flag appears after the end slash it will modify the way the regular expression works. The i flag will turn the case of a regular expression insensitive. For example, /aeiou/i will match both uppercase and lowercase vowels.

The g flag will specify a global match and that means that all matches of the pattern that has been specified are to be returned.

String Methods

A number of String methods will take a regular expression as an argument:

The search() Method

This method will take just one argument – a regular expression. The return is the index of the initial character of the substring that matches the regular expression. If there is no match, -1 is returned.

The split() Method

This method also take a regular expression and uses it as a delimiter to split one string into an array.

The replace() Method

This method will take two arguments – the regular expression and the string. The first regular expression match is replaced with the string and, if the g flag is used in the expression, all string matches will be replaced.

The match() Method

The `match()` method takes the regular expression as an argument and returns each of the substrings that are a match to the pattern of the regular expression.

Chapter 11: Regular Expressions – Syntax

Regular expressions are patterns that are used to specify a list of characters. In this chapter, we are going to look the syntax used to specify the characters:

Start and End (^ $)

- If there is a caret (^) at the start of a regular expression, it is an indicator that the string that is being researched has to begin with this pattern
- You will find pattern ^ in "food" but you won't find it in "barfood"
- If a regular expression has a dollar ($) sign at the end of it, it is an indication that the string that is being searched has to end with the pattern
- You will find pattern foo$ in "curfoo" but you won't find it in "food"

Number of Occurrences (? + * {})

These symbols will affect how many occurrences there are of the preceding character or, if you use parenthesis, characters - ?, *, +, {}

- The question mark (?) is an indication that the preceding character must appear 0 or 1 times in the pattern
- You will find pattern foo? In "fod" and "food" but not in "faod"

- The plus sign (+) is an indication that the preceding character will appear at least once in the pattern
- You will find pattern fo+ in "food", "fod" and "foood" but you won't find it in "fd"
- The asterisk (*) is an indicator that the preceding character has to appear at least 0 times in the pattern
- You will find pattern fo*d in "fd", "food" and "fod"
- The curly brackets ({}), with a single parameter {n} is an indicator that the preceding character must appear in the pattern exactly n times
- You will find pattern fo{3}d in "foood" but you won't find it in "fooood" or in "food"
- The curly brackets with two parameters {n1, n2} is an indicator that the previous character should appear in the pattern between n1 and n2 times
- You will find pattern fo{2,4} in "fooood", "foood" and in "food" but you won't find it in "foooood"
- Curly brackets that have one parameter with a second empty one {n} is an indicator that the previous character must appear in the pattern at least n times.

- You will find pattern fo{2} in "foooood" and in "food" but you won't find it in "fod"

Common Characters (. \d \D \w \W \s \S)

- A period (.) is representative of any character except for a newline
- You will find pattern fo.d in "foad", "food", "fo*f" and in "fo9d"
- The backslash-d (\d) is representative of any digit and is equivalent to [0-9]
- You will find the pattern fo\dd in "fo1d", food", fo4d" but you won't find it in "fodd" or in "food"
- The backslash-D (\D) is representative of any character with the exception of a digit and is the equivalent of [^0-9]
- You will find the pattern fo\D is "foad" and in "food" but you won't find it in "fo4d"
- The backslash-w is representative of any word character, such as digits, letters and underscore (_).
- You will find the pattern fo\w in "fo_d", "food" and in "fo4d" but you won't find it in "fo*d"
- The backslash-W (\W) is representative of any character that isn't a word character.

- "You can find the pattern fo\Wd in "fo&d", in "fo*d) and in "fo.d" but you won't find it in "fo d"
- The backslash-s (\s) character is representative of any whitespace character, such as tab, space, newline, etc.
- You will find pattern fo\sd in "fo d" but you won't find it in "food)
- The backslash-S (\S) is representative of any character except for a whitespace
- You can find the pattern fo\Sd in "food", in "fo*d" and in "fo4d" but you won't find it in "fo d"

Grouping ([])

We use square brackets ([]) as a way of grouping options together:

- You will find the pattern f[aeiou] in "fed" and "fad" but you won't find it in "food", "faed" or "fd".
- The pattern [aeiou] will match with "a", "e", "i", "o", or "u"
- You will find pattern f[aeiou]{2}d in "faed" and in "feod", but you won't find it in in "fod", "fed" or "fd".
- You will find the pattern [A-Za-z]+ in "Webucator, Inc.", but you won't find it in "13078".

- The pattern [A-Za-z] will match with any letter, regardless of whether it is upper or lowercase
- The pattern [A-Z] will match any letter that is uppercase
- The pattern [a-z] will match any letter that is lowercase

Negation (^)

When the caret (^) is used within square brackets and is the first character, it is indicative of negation

- You will find pattern f[^aeiou]d in "fqd" and "f4d", but you won't find it in "fad" or "fed".

Subpatterns (())

We use parentheses () to capture subpatterns

- You will find pattern f(oo)?d in "food" and "fd", but you won't find it in "fod".

Alternatives (|)

We use the pipe (|) as a way of creating optional patterns

- You will find pattern foo$|^bar in "foo" and "bar", but you won't find it in "foobar".

Escape Character (\ )

We use the backslash (\ ) as a way of escaping special characters.

- You will find pattern fo\.d in "fo.d", but you won't find it in "food" or "fo4d".

Chapter 12: Regular Expressions – Form Validation

When you use regular expressions, you can create some incredibly powerful functions that are for form validation. Have a look at this example:

Example:

RegularExpressions/Demos/Login.html

```
<!DOCTYPE HTML>

<html>

<head>

<meta charset="UTF-8">

<title>Login</title>

<script type="text/javascript">

var        reEmail        =        /^(\w+[\-
\.])*\w+@(\w+\.)+[A-Za-z]+$/;

var rePassword = /^[A-Za-z\d]{6,8}$/;


function validate(form){

    var email = form.Email.value;

    var password = form.Password.value;

    var errors = [];


    if (!reEmail.test(email)) {
```

```javascript
        errors[errors.length] = "You
must enter a valid email address.";

    }


    if (!rePassword.test(password)) {

        errors[errors.length] = "You
must enter a valid password.";

    }


    if (errors.length > 0) {

        reportErrors(errors);

        return false;

    }


    return true;

}


function reportErrors(errors){

    var msg = "There were some
problems...\n";

    for (var i = 0; i<errors.length;
i++) {

        var numError = i + 1;
```

```
                msg += "\n" + numError + ". "
+ errors[i];

      }

      alert(msg);

}

</script>

</head>

<body>

<h1>Login Form</h1>

<form method="post" action="Process.html"
onsubmit="return validate(this);">


      Email:        <input        type="text"
name="Email" size="25"><br/>

      Password:   <input    type="password"
name="Password" size="10"><br/>

      *Password must be between 6 and 10
characters and

      can   only   contain   letters   and
digits.<br/>


      <input                    type="submit"
value="Submit">

      <input   type="reset"   value="Reset
Form">
```

```
</p>

</form>

</body>

</html>
```

The code example start with the definition of a regular expression for an email address and one for a password as well so let's look at each one in turn:

```
var  reEmail  =  /^(\w+\.)*\w+@(\w+\.)+[A-Za-z]+$/;
```

- The caret (^) indicates that we should start at the beginning and this stops a user from inputting any invalid characters at the start of the email address.
- The pattern (\w+[\-\.])* indicates an allowance for a sequence of characters (word) that are followed by a dash or a dot. * is used as an indicator that the pattern may be repeated 0 times or more and successful patters will include: "ndunn.", "ndunn-", "nat.s.", and "nat-s-".
- The pattern \w+ will allow for a minimum of one word character
- @ will allow for one @ symbol.
- The pattern (\w+\.)+ will allow for a sequence of characters (word) that are followed by a dot. + is indicative of the

pattern being repeated at least once or more and this is the domain name minus the last bit, for example, .com
- The pattern [A-Za-z]+ will allow for at least one letter and is indicative of the last bit, for example, .com
- The dollar sign ($) indicates that you should end here. This stops a user from inputting invalid characters at the end of their email address

```
var rePassword = /^[A-Za-z\d]{6,8}$/;
```

- Same as above. The starting caret stops a user from inputting invalid characters at the start of the password
- The pattern [A-Za-z\d]{6,8} will allow for a sequence of digits and letter that is 6 to 8 characters' long
- Same as above, the dollar sign at the end stops a user from inputting an invalid character at the end of a password

Advanced Form Validation

This exercise should take you in the region of 25 to 40 minutes.

First Exercise

- Open RegularExpressions/Exercises/FormValidation.js in your editor.

Now write the correct regular expressions (additional ones) that will check for:

1. The proper name
   - That it begins with a capital letter
   - That it is followed by at least one letter or apostrophe
   - It may be more than one word, for example, "New Mexico"
2. Initial
   - That it has either 0 or 1 capital letter
3. State
   - That it has two capital letters
4. US Postal Code
   - That it is made up of five digits
   - May be followed with a dash and a further four digits
5. Username
   - That it is no less than 6 and no more than 15 digits or letters

Second Exercise

- Open RegularExpressions/Exercises/Register.html in your editor.

Add the correct validation for checking these fields:

- first name
- middle initial
- last name
- city
- state

- zip
- username

Test out your solution in your browser

A Challenge

Add in the correct regular expressions to test United Kingdom and Canadian postcodes:

- United Kingdom postcodes are two letters, one or two numbers, a whitespace, one number and two letters – for example WC12 3XY
- Canadian postcodes are one letter, one digit, one letter, a white pace, one digit, one letter and one digit – for example, M1A 2B3

Next make a modification to Register.html to check a postcode against these regular expressions as well as that of the US postcode.

Solution:

```
RegularExpressions/Solutions/FormValidati
on.js

//    Regular Expressions

var       reEmail    =      /^(\w+[\-
\.])*\w+@(\w+\.)+[A-Za-z]+$/;

var rePassword = /^[A-Za-z\d]{6,8}$/;

var  reProperName  =  /^([A-Z][A-Za-z']+
)*[A-Z][A-Za-z']+$/;

var reInitial = /^[A-Z]$/;
```

```javascript
var reState = /^[A-Z]{2}$/;

var rePostalUS = /^\d{5}(\-\d{4})?$/;

var reUsername = /^[A-Za-z\d]{6,15}$/;
```

Solution:

```html
<!DOCTYPE HTML>

<html>

<head>

<meta charset="UTF-8">

<title>Registration Form</title>

<script            type="text/javascript"
src="FormValidation.js"></script>

<script type="text/javascript">


function validate(form){

    var         firstName         =
form.FirstName.value;

    var         midInitial         =
form.MidInit.value;

    var lastName = form.LastName.value;

    var city = form.City.value;

    var state = form.State.value;

    var zipCode = form.Zip.value;

    var email = form.Email.value;
```

```javascript
var userName = form.Username.value;

var          password1          =
form.Password1.value;

var          password2          =
form.Password2.value;

var errors = [];



if  (!reProperName.test(firstName))
{

        errors[errors.length]  =  "You
must enter a valid first name.";

    }



if (!reInitial.test(midInitial)) {

        errors[errors.length]  =  "You
must enter a one-letter middle initial.";

    }



if (!reProperName.test(lastName)) {

        errors[errors.length]  =  "You
must enter a valid last name.";

    }



if (!reProperName.test(city)) {
```

```
            errors[errors.length] = "You
must enter a valid city.";

        }


        if (!reState.test(state)) {

            errors[errors.length] = "You
must enter a valid state.";

        }


        if (!rePostalUS.test(zipCode)) {

            errors[errors.length] = "You
must enter a valid zip code.";

        }


        if (!reUsername.test(userName)) {

            errors[errors.length] = "You
must enter a valid username.";

        }
```

Challenge Solution:

```
RegularExpressions/Solutions/FormValidati
on-challenge.js

//    Regular Expressions


var rePostalUS = /^\d{5}(\-\d{4})?$/;
```

```
var rePostalCA = /^[A-Z]\d[A-Z] \d[A-
Z]\d$/;

var rePostalUK = /^[A-Z]{2}[0-9]{1,2}
?[0-9]{1}[A-Z]{2}$/;
```

Challenge Solution:

```
<!DOCTYPE HTML>

<html>

<head>

<meta charset="UTF-8">

<title>Registration Form</title>

<script          type="text/javascript"
src="FormValidation-
challenge.js"></script>

<script type="text/javascript">


function validate(form){


    if (!rePostalUS.test(zipCode)

            &&
!rePostalCA.test(zipCode)

            &&
!rePostalUK.test(zipCode))

    {

        errors[errors.length] = "You
must enter a valid postal code.";
```

```
        }


    return true;
}
```

Chapter 13: Cleaning Up Form Entries

Sometimes it is nice to clean user entries as soon as they are input and we can do this by using a combination of the replace() method of string objects and regular expressions.

The `replace()` Method Revisited

We already looked at this method and how to use it to replace a regular expression match with a string but we can also use it together with backreferences and replace a pattern that has been matched with a brand-new string that is made from substrings of that pattern. The following example shows you this:

Example:

```
<!DOCTYPE HTML>

<html>

<head>

<meta charset="UTF-8">

<title>ssn Cleaner</title>

<script type="text/javascript">

var reSSN = /^(\d{3})[\-  ]?(\d{2})[\-
]?(\d{4})$/;


function cleanSsn(ssn){

    if (reSSN.test(ssn)) {
```

```
        var         cleanedSsn        =
ssn.replace(reSSN, "$1-$2-$3");

        return cleanedSsn;

    } else {

        alert("INVALID SSN");

        return ssn;

    }

}

</script>

</head>

<body>

    <form onsubmit="return false;">

        <input type="text" name="ssn"
size="20">

        <input           type="button"
value="Clean SSN"

    onclick="this.form.ssn.value      =
cleanSsn(this.form.ssn.value);">

    </form>

</body>

</html>
```

We use the `cleanSsn()` function to clean a social security number in this example. In reSSN, ^(\d{3})[\-]?(\d{2})[\-]?(\d{4})$, the regular expression has three separate subexpressions: (\d{3}), (\d{2}), and (\d{4}). These can be referenced as $1, $2, and $3, respectively in the `replace()` method.

When a user clicks the button that says "Clean SSN" , they call the `cleanSsn()` function This function will then test to see of the number input by the user is a valid number and, if it is, it will then clean it using the code below – this code will dash-delimit the substrings that match the subexpressions:

```
var cleanedSsn = ssn.replace(reSSN, "$1-$2-$3");
```

The properly cleaned social security number will then be returned

Cleaning Up Form Entries

This exercise should take you about 15 to 25 minutes.

- Open RegularExpressions/Exercises/PhoneCleaner.html in your editor
- Where it is indicated by the comment, you must declare a variable called `cleanedPhone` and then assign it a cleaned version of the phone number entered by the user. The clean version should be in this format – (111) 222 3333
- Test out your solution in your browser

A Challenge

You sometimes find a phone number is a combination of numbers and letters and some of these have an extra character in them to complete the word. Your challenge is to add in a function that is named `convertPhone()`. This function will:

- Strip out every character that is not a letter or a number
- Convert every letter to a number as per the following list:
  - ABC -> 2
  - DEF -> 3
  - GHI -> 4
  - JKL -> 5
  - MNO -> 6
  - PQRS -> 7
  - TUV -> 8
  - WXYZ -> 9

It must also:

- Pass the initial 10 characters of the string that results to the function `cleanPhone()`
- Return the string result
- Then modify the form, calling `convertPhone()` and not `cleanPhone()`
- Test the solution in your browser

Solution:

```
<!DOCTYPE HTML>
```

```html
<html>

<head>

<meta charset="UTF-8">

<title>Phone Cleaner</title>

<script type="text/javascript">

var rePhone = /^\(?([2-9]\d\d)\)?[\-\.
]?([2-9]\d\d)[\-\. ]?(\d{4})$/;


function cleanPhone(phone){

    if (rePhone.test(phone)) {

        var cleanedPhone =
phone.replace(rePhone, "($1) $2-$3");

        return cleanedPhone;

    } else {

        alert("INVALID PHONE");

        return phone;

    }

}


</script>

</head>

<body>

    <form onsubmit="return false;">
```

```
            <input                 type="text"
name="Phone" size="20">

            <input                 type="button"
value="Convert Phone"

    onclick="this.form.Phone.value      =
cleanPhone(this.form.Phone.value);">

    </form>

</body>

</html>
```

Challenge Solution:

```
<!DOCTYPE HTML>

<html>

<head>

<meta charset="UTF-8">

<title>Phone Checker</title>

<script type="text/javascript">

var    rePhone   =   /^\(?([2-9]\d\d)\)?[\-\.
]?([2-9]\d\d)[\-\. ]?(\d{4})$/;




function convertPhone(phone){

    var convertedPhone;
```

```
        convertedPhone                      =
phone.replace(/[^A-Za-z\d]/g, "");

        convertedPhone                      =
convertedPhone.replace(/[ABC]/gi, "2");

        convertedPhone                      =
convertedPhone.replace(/[DEF]/gi, "3");

        convertedPhone                      =
convertedPhone.replace(/[GHI]/gi, "4");

        convertedPhone                      =
convertedPhone.replace(/[JKL]/gi, "5");

        convertedPhone                      =
convertedPhone.replace(/[MNO]/gi, "6");

        convertedPhone                      =
convertedPhone.replace(/[PQRS]/gi, "7");

        convertedPhone                      =
convertedPhone.replace(/[TUV]/gi, "8");

        convertedPhone                      =
convertedPhone.replace(/[WXYZ]/gi, "9");

        return
cleanPhone(convertedPhone.substr(0, 10));

    }

</script>

</head>

<body>

    <form onsubmit="return false;">

        <input                type="text"
name="Phone" size="20">
```

```
        <input                type="button"
value="Convert  Phone"


    onclick="this.form.Phone.value    =
convertPhone(this.form.Phone.value);">

    </form>

</body>

</html>
```

Bonus Chapter: Working with AJAX

AJAX stands for Asynchronous JavaScript and XML and it is a group of technologies, such as DOM, JavaScript, HTML, XML and CSS, that are all inter-related. AJAX lets you send data and receive it asynchronously without having to reload your web page, making it incredibly fast.

AJAX also allows you to send only the most important information to the web server and not the whole page so only the valuable data will be routed over to the client side. This makes any application you build and use a good deal faster and more interactive. AJAX is used on a very large number of web applications, including Facebook, Gmail, Google Maps, Twitter, and too many more to mention.

How Does AJAX Work?

When you use the traditional JavaScript code and you want to get some information out of a server file or a database, or if you wanted to send some information over to a server, you would make an HTML form and you would use POST or GET to send or receive data to and from a data. End users would need to click a button that says SUBMIT to send or get the answer; they would then have to wait while the server responded and then a new page would load up with their results.

Each time input is submitted by a user, a new page is returned by the server and, because of this, some web applications run quite slowly and are not always very user-friendly. When you use AJAX, JavaScript will talk straight to the server via the JavaScript object `XMLHttpRequest`.

By using an HTTP request, web pages can request and receive a response form web servers without the need to reload the page. The users stay on the same page and will not have a clue that there are scripts sending requests for pages or sending data to a server as this will be working away in the background.

The user will send a request that will, in turn, execute an action. The response to this action will be shown into a layer, identified via an ID and all without the page having to go through a full reload. This is an example of a page ID:

```
<div id="ajaxResponse"></div>
```

Next, we are going to look briefly at how to create the `XMLHttpRequest` object and get responses from the server:

Step 1: Create the object `XMLHttpRequest`.

Every different browser will use a different method to create this object; Internet Explorer makes use of ActiveXObject while some of the other browsers use `XMLHttpRequest`, which is, of course, the built-in object in JavaScript.

To create the object and to deal with all the different browsers, we are going to make use of a statement called "catch and try"

```
function ajaxFunction()
{
var xmlHttp;
try
{
// Firefox, Opera 8.0+, Safari
xmlHttp=new XMLHttpRequest();
}
catch (e)
{
// Internet Explorer
try
{
xmlHttp=new
ActiveXObject("Msxml2.XMLHTTP");
}
catch (e)
{
try
{
xmlHttp=new
ActiveXObject("Microsoft.XMLHTTP");
}
catch (e)
{
alert("Your browser does not support
AJAX!");
return false;
}
}
}
```

Step 2: Sending the Request to a Server

To send the request to a server, we will use the methods `open()` and `send()`

The first method will take three arguments – the first to define the method used when the GET or POST request is sent, the second to specify the URL of the script on the server side and the third to specify that the request must be asynchronously handled. The second method is used to send the request over to the server.

```
xmlHttp.open("GET","time.asp",true);
xmlHttp.send(null);
```

Step 3: Writing the Server Side Script

`responseText` is going to store any data that is returned from a server and we want to send the current time back. For this we will use time.asp and the code will look like this:

```
<%
response.expires=-1
response.write(time)
%>
```

Step 4: Consuming the Response

The next step is to consume whatever response comes back and then display it to the end user:

```
xmlHttp.onreadystatechange=function()
{
```

```
if(xmlHttp.readyState==4)
{
document.myForm.time.value=xmlHttp.respon
seText;
}
}
xmlHttp.open("GET","time.asp",true);
xmlHttp.send(null);
}
```

Step 5: Completing the Code

The final step is to determine when we should execute the AJAX function. This is going to run in the background whenever a user inputs something into a text field for the username and the entire code would look like this:

```
<html>
<body>

<script type="text/javascript">
function ajaxFunction()
{
var xmlHttp;
try
{
// Firefox, Opera 8.0+, Safari
xmlHttp=new XMLHttpRequest();
}
catch (e)
{
// Internet Explorer
try
{
xmlHttp=new
ActiveXObject("Msxml2.XMLHTTP");
}
```

```
catch (e)
{
try
{
xmlHttp=new
ActiveXObject("Microsoft.XMLHTTP");
}
catch (e)
{
alert("Your browser does not support
AJAX!");
return false;
}
}
}
xmlHttp.onreadystatechange=function()
{
if(xmlHttp.readyState==4)
{
document.myForm.time.value=xmlHttp.respon
seText;
}
}
xmlHttp.open("GET","time.asp",true);
xmlHttp.send(null);
}
</script>
<form name="myForm">
Name: <input type="text"
onkeyup="ajaxFunction();" name="username"
/>
Time: <input type="text" name="time" />
</form>
</body>
</html>
```

That is a basic look at how AJAX works and
what it can do. There is plenty of information

available on the internet for you to research
this further but do ensure you are familiar with
advanced JavaScript first.

Conclusion

Thank you again for reading this book!

I hope this book was able to help you to understand and grasp some of the more advanced techniques in JavaScript and I hope that you found the exercises useful – they are designed to test your knowledge and also to help you learn much quicker. It is always better to learn from practical examples, especially with computer program languages, rather than just reading and trying to take it in.

The next step is to practice. It doesn't matter how much you have read or how much you have learned to date; if you don't practice you will soon lose it. The nature of computer programming is that things change on a regular basis. Keep up your learning otherwise you will have to go back to basics!

Finally, if this book has given you value and helped you in any way, then I'd like to ask you for a favor, if you would be kind enough to leave a review for this book on Amazon? It'd be greatly appreciated!

Thank you and good luck!

Java:

Advanced Guide to Programming Code with Java

Charlie Masterson

Introduction

I want to thank you and congratulate you for downloading the book, *"Java: Advanced Guide to Programming Code with Java"*.

This book contains proven steps and strategies on how to advance your Java programming skills and is not for those who have little or no knowledge about the computer programming knowledge. If you are new to it, please learn the basics of Java programming before you attempt the chapters in this book as, otherwise they will mean nothing to you.

Java is one of the more popular of the computer programming languages and is commonly used in building websites, web services and Android as well as being the basis of an awful lot of enterprise systems. Another good thing about Java is that it works cross-platform and we're not just talking computers here. Many of your household appliances actually run on the Java environment and that means the possibilities are endless.

Thanks again for downloading this book, I hope you enjoy it and I hope that you gain a lot from it!

Chapter 1:
Java Generic
Programming

Wouldn't it be nice, and so much easier if we were able to write just one sort method that was able to sort out the elements that were in any array of any type that supported ordering, like a String array or an Integer array, for example? That is where Java Generic classes and methods come into play.

These generic methods and classes let you use just one method declaration to specify a set of methods that are related, or just one class declaration to specify a set of types that were related. Generics also give you a compile-time safety that lets you catch any invalid types when it comes to compiling time.

By using the Java Generic concept, you can write one method that will sort an object array, invoke the method using String arrays, Double arrays, Integer arrays, and so on, to sort the elements in the array.

Generic Methods

As a coder, you can write one method declaration that you can call using arguments of all different types. Based on which argument types are passed to the method the compiler will handle each call in the appropriate way. These are the rules that define Generic methods:

- Every generic method declaration must contain a section for type parameters that is delimited with the use of angle brackets (<>). This section must precede the return type of the method (in the example that follows later, that will be type <E>).

- Each section of type parameters must have at least one type parameter in it and each parameter must be separated by a comma. You may know type parameters better as type variables and these are identifiers used to specify the name of a generic type.

- Type parameters are used to declare return types and are also used as placeholders for the argument types that are passed to the method – these are known as type arguments.

- The body of a generic method is declared in the same way as any other method. Do note that a type parameter can only represent reference types and cannot be used for primitive types, like `double, int and char`

Example

This example shows you how to use a Generic method to print an array that contains different types:

```
public class GenericMethodTest {
   // generic method printArray
   public static < E > void printArray(
E[] inputArray ) {
      // This displays the array elements
      for(E element : inputArray) {
         System.out.printf("%s             ",
element);
      }
      System.out.println();
   }

   public static void main(String args[])
{
      // This creates arrays of Integer,
Double and Character
      Integer[] intArray = { 1, 2, 3, 4,
5 };
      Double[] doubleArray = { 1.1, 2.2,
3.3, 4.4 };
      Character[] charArray = { 'H', 'E',
'L', 'L', 'O' };

      System.out.println("Array
integerArray contains:");
      printArray(intArray);    // pass an
Integer array

      System.out.println("\nArray
doubleArray contains:");
      printArray(doubleArray);    // pass
a Double array
```

```
        System.out.println("\nArray
characterArray contains:");
        printArray(charArray);     // pass a
Character array
    }
}
```

The output of this example would be:

The Array `integerArray` contains:

```
1 2 3 4 5
```

The Array `doubleArray` contains:

```
1.1 2.2 3.3 4.4
```

The Array `characterArray` contains:

```
H E L L O
```

Bounded Type Parameters

On occasion, you may want to be able to restrict what kinds of type can be passed to the type parameter. For example, you may have a method that operates only on numbers and you might want it to only accept `Number` instances or subclasses of `Number` and this is where bounded type parameters come in.

To declare one of these bounded type parameters, you must list the name of the type parameter, then the keyword extends and then the upper bound.

Example

This example shows you how to use the extends keyword in a general way, to mean **extends** (in the case of classes) or **implements** (in the case of interfaces). This is a Generic method that will return the biggest of a set of three Comparable objects:

```
public class MaximumTest {
    // this determines the biggest of
three Comparable objects

    public static <T extends
Comparable<T>> T maximum(T x, T y, T z) {
        T max = x;    // assumes x is the
biggest to start with

        if(y.compareTo(max) > 0) {
            max = y;    // y is the biggest
so far
        }

        if(z.compareTo(max) > 0) {
            max = z;    // z is the biggest
now
        }
        return max;        // returns the
biggest object
    }

    public static void main(String args[])
{
```

```
      System.out.printf("Max   of   %d,   %d
and %d is %d\n\n",
         3, 4, 5, maximum( 3, 4, 5 ));

      System.out.printf("Max   of  %.1f,%.1f
and %.1f is %.1f\n\n",
            6.6,   8.8,   7.7,   maximum(  6.6,
8.8, 7.7 ));

      System.out.printf("Max   of   %s,   %s
and %s is %s\n","pear",
         "apple",                    "orange",
maximum("pear", "apple", "orange"));
   }
}
```

This will give you the following output:

```
Max of 3, 4 and 5 is 5

Max of 6.6,8.8 and 7.7 is 8.8

Max of pear, apple, and orange is pear
```

Generic Classes

Generic class declarations look very similar to those that are non-generic with one exception – the class name must be followed by the name of the type parameter. In the same way that we did with generic methods, in the generic classes, the type parameter section can contain one or more type parameters, each one separated by a comma. These are otherwise known as parameterized types or parameterized classes because they are able to take one or more parameters.

Example

This example shows you how to define a generic class:

```java
public class Box<T> {
   private T t;

   public void add(T t) {
      this.t = t;
   }

   public T get() {
      return t;
   }

   public static void main(String[] args)
{
      Box<Integer>    integerBox    =    new
Box<Integer>();
      Box<String>    stringBox    =    new
Box<String>();

      integerBox.add(new Integer(10));
      stringBox.add(new        String("Hello
World"));

      System.out.printf("Integer      Value
:%d\n\n", integerBox.get());
      System.out.printf("String      Value
:%s\n", stringBox.get());
   }
}
```

This will give you this result:

```
Integer Value :10
String Value :Hello World
```

Chapter 2: Java Collections– Array Lists and HashMaps

Have you ever seen a TreeSet, a HashMap or an ArrayList in Java code and wondered what on earth they are? Java collections are incredibly important tools that we use to store some of the more dynamic data types. But, what if you are not aware of just how much data there is going to be beforehand? What if the data type that you are looking to store isn't a basic data type? What I mean by that is, what if you wanted to store a whole lot of Cat objects, for example? Yes, you could use an array but you may not know how many Cat objects you have beforehand. And what if you wanted to create some kind of relationship between the data, for example linking a text string to a specific object?

Let's look into Java Collections and see what they are and how you use them.

ArrayList

Let's assume that you have created a simulation of a planet and the alien population of that planet just keeps on growing. If Alien is an object, how many of these Alien objects will be present by the time the simulation ends? What about if you wanted the simulation to run and never stop? You can't possibly know how many Alien objects there are going to be before you create an array to store them in. In all honesty, you could nothing more than just hazard a guess and that, in Java, is totally unacceptable.

If there is one very useful tool in Java it is the ArrayList object, nothing more than a dynamic array. When this object is created, you will not specify any size for it. Let me see if I can make that any clearer – THERE IS NO NEED FOR YOU TO SPECIFY THE SIZE OF THE ARRAYLIST! The ArrayList is an array that is empty to start with.

So, what does this ArrayList look like? This is a little tricky – ArrayLists can store just about anything so you have to be sure to tell it exactly what it is going to store. Let me show you a quick example – the ArrayList is going to be used to store Integers. A quick note here – an Integer and an int are not the same thing – Integers are objects and ints are primitive data types. That said, they are handled similarly by Java

```
ArrayList<Integer>    array    =    new
ArrayList<Integer>();
```

If you are using Eclipse, a red line will appear underneath ArrayList, telling you that ArrayList has to be imported first. Here is the import statement:

```
import java.util.ArrayList;
```

How do you add the values that you want to be stored? This is an example of how to add an item to the end of the ArrayList:

```
array.add(1);
```

What if you wanted to remove an item from the ArrayList? That's no problem either when you use this example. Just make sure that you provide the position in the Array of the item that is to be removed:

```
array.remove(0);
```

This will remove the 0th element that is in the array, in simple terms, the first element in Java. Remember, the first line is always numbered 0. If you wanted to remove an element that was somewhere in the middle, the list will shorten itself automatically so that there are no gaps.

Ok, so how do we access a specific element from the list? That too is relatively simple:

```
array.get(0);
```

Once you get the hang of ArrayLists, you will discover just how powerful they are and you will find that you use them instead of regular arrays.

HashMap

There is far more to a Java Collection than just making better arrays, though. We also have the HashMap. This is a one-on-one relationship that takes place between two objects. Let me try and explain that a little better for those who really don't like Math!

Let's assume that you need to get into your email account You can't do this straightaway and you are taken first to a login screen. Here, you input your username and your password and, provided you input the right combination, you can go to your account.

HashMaps work in a similar way – the input has to be appropriate to generate the correct output. Each input will be mapped to just one output and, in the example I used above, the correct username and password (the input) produce the output of you being able to access your email account. Let's look at an example of code:

```
HashMap<String,    String>    map    =    new
HashMap<String, String>();
```

Again, there is an import statement missing but you can get the required import by typing in:

```
import java.util.NameOfObject
```

For `NameOfObject`, input the Collection, HashMap in this case. You could also just press the key combination Ctrl+Shift+O to import everything automatically when you use Eclipse.

So, take another look at the HashMap above and you will notice `<String, String>`. What this means is that the key, which is the first value, is a `String`, as is the second value. Of course, you can have any object combination that you choose.

The key is used to obtain its value and one key will correspond to just one value, the same as an email username corresponds to a single password. Inserting a new key or value pair is easy:

```
map.put ("Me", "Password");
```

And to delete:

```
map.remove ("Me");
```

If you wanted to have an array that stored all of the keys that are in the HashMap, you could use the `keySet()` method, as such:

```
String[]  keys  =  map.keySet()  .toArray
(new String[map.size()]);
```

This is somewhat tricky. The `keySet()` method will return a `Set` which is then, in turn, made into a `String` array by the creation of a new `String` with a length the same as the HashMap size. That array will then be stored into an array with the name of keys. We have created a `String` array because the keys are all `Strings` from earlier.

So, how are HashMaps going to be useful? Simply because they allow you to store objects rather than index values like you do with the ArrayList. With the above example, you could look through the HashMap to find a password by using the key, which would be the username.

A note – you cannot store any primitive data types inside an ArrayList, a HashMap or any other Collection in Java. A Java Collection may only be used to store objects and this is a very important point so please try to remember it.

This has been an introduction to advanced collection types, some incredibly powerful Java tools that, when you use them properly can make the capabilities of your program far more effective. There are more than I have talked about but these are the important ones. I would, however, stress that you should learn the others as well and apply them in the programs you write.

Chapter 3:
Java Inheritance

In order to understand Java Inheritance, you have to have a thorough understanding of objects first; if you haven't, go back and learn them before you carry on.

So, by now, you should have been using objects and classes as representations of different bits of your program code. For example, you could create a Dog class that makes Dog objects, each of which has the characteristics of a Dog. You could also make a Cat class, in the same way, one that makes Cat objects with the characteristics of Cats and a Bird Class that makes Bird objects with the characteristics of birds. If you think about it, there will be some characteristics that are similar between all of the objects and the code will be duplicated in each class.

So, what if I was to tell you that you could make one single Animal object that would complete all of this for you? Well you can, using Java Inheritance:

Superclass

The first thing to consider when we talk about Java inheritance is the superclass. This is pretty much the same as a normal class in Java but with the exception that we now know we will want other classes to be created from that object. We are not going to worry about how we do that at this moment, first of all, we are going to look at what a superclass looks like:

```
public class Animal {
}
```

Hold on; doesn't a superclass look just like any other class? Yes, it does. Any superclass can look just the same as any regular class so the real magic of the superclass is actually in the subclass.

Subclass

The subclass is the child of the parent class. In essence, they are derived from their superclass. Using the superclass above, this is a subclass:

```
public class Dog extends Animal {
}
```

Note the new keyword here, one that is used when the class is created – `extends`. This is the keyword used to declare that a class is a subclass of another specified class. Please note that you can only extend one single class.

An Animal Example

So, what is the real point of Java inheritance? The point is, you can use to cut down on the amount of code you need to write and you can make that code seem more real-world with

Java inheritance. Let's go back to our cat and dog objects. Both of these are animals so we could come up with a superclass that we call Animal – this will define the characteristics of all types of animals and would then create the special characteristics that go with a cat and a dog.

Let's begin with the superclass, Animal. We can create methods and variables that all of the animals will have but, for now, we are going to keep it quite simple with two variables and two methods that all animals will have. Look at the code:

```java
public class Animal {
      public boolean isAPet = true
      public String owner = "Bob";

      public void sleep () {
            System.out.println
("Sleeping");
      }
      public void eat () {
            System.out.println
("Eating");
      }
}
```

Here we have created a set of basic methods and variables that all the animals are going to have; in this example, the animals will have a boolean named isAPet, set to true. The owner has a value of `Bob` and is set as a String while all of the animals will all eat and sleep.

Now that what all of the animals will do is defined, we can begin to create the subclasses. We already had a Dog subclass that we created earlier so we will just make use of that here. This is an empty class but it already has full access to any of the protected or public methods from the superclass. Look at the example:

```
public static void main (String[] args) {
       Dog d = new Dog();
       d.sleep();
}
```

Did you notice that there are no errors? This is because our superclass shares the protected and pubic methods and variables with its subclasses.

So, you could possibly be wondering what protected and public are. These are access level modifiers, tow of the three that are used in Java. You have more than likely seen public quite a bit but protected will be something new to you. What is important at this stage is that these are the only two modifiers that will let a subclass use the variables and methods from the superclass.

Now we can create more specific code for Dog objects, let's create a method called bark:

```
public class Dog extends Animal {
    public void bark() {
        System.out.println("Woof");
    }
}
```

Because it is only Dos that bark, the subclass contains the method and the superclass will have no access to that method at all.

Now it's time to create the Cat class, another subclass of Animal superclass:

```
public class Cat extends Animal {
}
```

This is also empty but, like Dog, it has access to the methods and variables in the superclass. Now we can create a method called meow:

```
public class cat extends animal {
    public void meow() {
        system.out.println("meow!");
    }
}
```

Like Bark exists only in the Dog class, Meow will only exist in the Cat class. Neither Dogs nor the superclass will have any access to the method and this is why Java inheritance is one of the most powerful concepts in the language

– quite simply, the incredible ability to define common methods and variables in one place and use them over and over.

Abstract Methods and Classes

Both classes and methods may be declared as abstract – abstract methods don't have any implementation and abstract classes are not able to be made into objects. This will mean more if you look at the code example that uses the Animal class we made earlier:

```
public abstract class Animal {
      public boolean isAPet = true;
      public String owner = "Bob";
      public void sleep() {

      System.out.println("Sleeping");
      }
      public void eat() {
            System.out.println("Eating");
      }
}
```

Now, because this is an abstract class, we cannot do Animal a = new Animal();. However, aside from that, this class can be defined in the same way that we define any other class but with one more exception – now, you can't create any Animal – you are now forcing yourself into creating specifics, like Dog and Cat.

Perhaps the more interesting part of inheritance is the abstract method. With this, you can create your method but you don't need to fill in any code inside it! The following is an example – we are going to add an abstract method to the Animal class using the method of `move()`

```
public abstract class Animal {
      public boolean isAPet = true;
      public String owner = "Bob";
      public void sleep() {

      System.out.println("Sleeping");
      }
      public void eat() {
            System.out.println("Eating");
      }
      public abstract void move();
}
```

Note – it is very important that curly brackets are NOT used with abstract methods. You must also remember that a semicolon has to be placed at the end of the line just as if you were writing normal code.

So, what can be done with abstract methods that are empty? The answer comes from the subclasses. Because these are abstract methods in the superclass, the subclass has to implement the methods. This means that the subclass decides what code must go in the method and the method must exist in the subclass. Let's show you how powerful this can be – we are going to implement the move() method in the Dog and Cat classes:

```java
public class Dog extends Animal {
      public void bark() {
            System.out.println("Woof!");
      }
      public void move() {

      System.out,println("Running");
      }
}

public class Cat extends Animal {
      public void meow() {
            System.out.println ("Meow!");
      }
      public void move() {
            System.out.println
("Prancing");
      }
}
```

Now all the animals can use the same methods but will perform them in different ways. Note – if the abstract methods that are from the superclass are not implemented in the subclasses, the subclasses will throw up errors – remember, all abstract methods MUST be implemented.

This should give you a basic understanding of what Java Inheritance is and how to use it. I don't expect you to get it straight away; have a play around with extending classes and abstract classes. See what you can and can't do. Have a go at extending a class that extends another class and see what will happen. Experiment, it's the best way to learn!

Chapter 4:
Java Interface

The Java Interface is much the same as a Java class type that we talked about in the last chapter – Java Inheritance. When we talked about inheritance, we looked at a new keyword that we used in front of the word class right at the beginning of the class file. That keyword was abstract and we used it to create classes that could not be turned into objects. Now we are going to look at a brand-new type of file, the Java Interface. By the end of this chapter, you will begin to see how much structure you can give your program through the correct use of the Java interface.

What is the Java Interface?

It is important for you to understand that the Java Interface is neither object nor class. It is, is a kind of blueprint for classes but, on its own, it is not comprised of classes. This is the main difference between the Interface and an abstract class, which, as you know, is a class but you can't make it into an object. Likewise, the Java Interface also can't be turned into an object. Let's make things a little clearer with an example of what a Java Interface looks like:

```
public interface InterfaceExample {
    public void hi();
    public String getName();
    public int add (int a, int b);
}
```

Did you notice that there is no code in ANY of the methods and that each one has a semicolon at the end? The abstract is the only other method type that can end in a semicolon and not have any code and the abstract method belongs to the abstract class. In a Java Interface, you must remember that you cannot implement any of the methods and each must have a semicolon at the end of it. Why? Because it is NOT a class.

Note: The way to create an Interface is pretty much the same way as you so a class – the file name must end in .java and it must be the same name as the Interface, right down to capitalization – they must be exactly the same.

OK, we have Java file, an interface that doesn't have any working code in it so, what do we do with it? What is the point of it? To explain this better, we must go back to the abstract class. Remember, to use the abstract class we had to use the keyword extends. Look at this example:

```
public class dog extends Animal {
}
```

Did you notice that Dog extends Animal? What does that mean? It means that Dog is a subclass of the class Animal and all of its functionality comes from Animal. Now, let's

make a new abstract class and let's call it
FourLeggedObject:

```
public    class    FourLeggedObject    extends
Animal {
}
```

Now I want to use the Dog class to extend
FourLeggedObject. Not going to happen! Why
not? Because it is impossible. Why? Why can't
an object extend whatever classes it wants to?
For a very good reason, - Java is simply not
able to handle multiple inheritances and that is
exactly what this would cause.

How to Use the Java Interface

Although Java is not able to handle multiple
inheritances it has kind of got around it by
using Java Interface. The Interface is incredibly
useful in that you can use objects to implement
multiple or single interfaces. This means that
your object will conform to several different
Interface types. Here is an example showing
the   Dog   class   implementing   multiple
interfaces:

```
public   class   Dog   implements   Animal,
FourLeggedObject {
}
```

If you wanted to add one interface you would
declare it but if you wanted several, you just

declare them all with a comma separating each one. It really is as simple as that. However, in case you hadn't realized, the Dog class now has no choice but to implement all of the methods in Animal and in FourLeggedObject. That is the point of the Java Interface – to give you, the programmer, a "blueprint" that lets you create the object. Please note that you don't have to implement only the methods that are defined within the Interface; you can add new methods into your class in addition to the ones that you have got to have.

Note: if an error appears in your class, go back and make sure that all of the methods have been implemented in every interface that is being implemented. Also, check that the signatures are the same – return type, accessor type, capitalization of names, etc.

Java Interfaces have another benefit – the ability to put objects into collections that have different object types in them. Remember when we discussed Java Collections, a couple of chapters back? One collection that you can do this with is the ArrayList and that can be used to store specific object types. Let's look at an example where we store a group of Animals. We are going to see how Dog will implement Animal, which means that Dog is an Animal:

```
import java.util.ArrayList;
```

```
public class DogStoreExample {
     public static void main (String[]
args) {
          Dog d = new Dog();
          ArrayList<Animal>    animals    -
new ArrayList<Animal>();


     }
}
```

A collection can be told to store a group of objects based on the type of Interface, So, you don't have to store just Dogs in the ArrayList for animals you can also put them into another ArrayList – FourLeggedObject:

```
import java.util.ArrayList;
public class DogStoreExample {
     public static void main (String[]
args) {
          Dog d = new Dog();
          ArrayList<Animal>    animals    =
new ArrayLIst<Animal>();
          animals.add(d);
          ArrayList<FourLeggedObject>
          fourLeggedObjects    =    new
          ArrayList<FourLeggedObject>()
          ;
          fourLeggedObjects.add (d);
     }
}
```

What this means is that objects can be mixed and matched based entirely on the fact that they have got the same Interface. So, now we are going to store another object in the

ArrayList FourLeggedObject, a chair this time (they have four legs, don't they?):

```
public      class      Chair      implements
FourLeggedObject {
}
import java.util.ArrayList;
public class DoStoreExample {
     public static void main (String[]
args) {
          Dog d = new Dog();
          ArrayList<Animal>  animals  =
new ArrayList<Animal>();
          animals.add (d);
          ArrayList<FourLeggedObject>
          fourLeggedObjects    -    new
          ArrayList<FourLeggedObject>()
          ;
          Chair c = new Chair();
          fourLeggedObjects.add ©;
     }
}
```

Now we have Chairs and Dogs in the same ArrayList because the objects we are storing are all of the type FourLeggedObject and both of the objects are FourLeggedObjects. Don't you think this is much better than having a separate ArrayList for each object type?

Have a go at using the Java Interface in the code you write. It can be of great help to start you off on creating an object when you are not quite sure how that object should be implemented – because an interface has no implementation! You can use them as building blocks if you like and I would recommend that you get to grips with these and use them to make your life easier.

In the next chapter, we are going to look at Polymorphism. Not sure what that is? Best read on then and learn how polymorphism can be used to help you create the best object-oriented Java applications.

Chapter 5:
Java
Polymorphism

Polymorphism is best described as the bread and butter of object-oriented Java programming. So, what is polymorphism and what do you use it for? In short, it can help you to create some very clear and elegant code but it is a little more difficult than other concepts because it is more abstract than many other Java concepts. However, master this and you will be well on the way to be a great programmer and will find it a lot easier to grasp and master Java programming.

What is Polymorphism?

If you want to properly grasp Java, you must master the concept of polymorphism. In simple terms, polymorphism is the concept that lets actions act in a different way based on the type of object that is performing the action or the type of object that the action is performed on. Let's use a very simple example to demonstrate that – the sound that a cat makes. We know it is meow so this action is going to be called `makeSound()`. Remember, methods can be used to represent actions.

Now, the sound that a dog makes is woof so this action can also be called `makeSound()`. In fact, let's just say, for the sake of simplicity, that all animals `makeSound()`. As such, `makeSound()` will do something different, depending on the animals. In other words, the action will act differently based on the object type.

Look, although it may seem somewhat complicated, polymorphism isn't hard at all. Different animals will make different sounds and you can use the same method for each sound. If you understood Java Inheritance, you will understand this.

One of the most powerful ways to use polymorphic behavior is to use the same method mane, over and over in the same class to get the result you want. So how does polymorphism do this?

Overloaded Methods

Let's use the `makeSound()` example. A dog will woof but, if it has an injury, it might whimper instead. How do we use that `makeSound()` method for both sounds? Look at this example:

```
public class Dog extends Animal {
     public void makeSound() {
          System.out.println("Woof!");
     }
     public    void    makeSound(boolean
injured) {
     }
}
```

Right now, if you still don't fully understand the code example, you really should go back and go over methods again and then come back.

Back to the example: we can see that, depending on how many parameters are passed to makeSound(), the dog will make a different sound. But, hold on! Why couldn't we just use an if statement and make this into one method? We could have done and that may have been the best way for this particular example but then you wouldn't have known how to do it. Let's say, though, that an external action makes the difference in the sound, a bit like this:

```
public void makeSound(boolean injured) {
     if (injured) {

     System.out.println("Whimper");
     }
}
```

If there was no variable for the dog to know that it had been hurt, there is no way you could have written the if statement quite so easily. You can overload methods as much as you want provided the number of parameters or the types of parameter are all different. For example, you couldn't do this:

```
public void makeSound(int x, int y) {
```

```
}
public void makeSound(int dog, int cat) {
}
```

The reason this doesn't work is because there is the same type of parameters and the same number of parameters.

Overridden Methods

In Java, it is possible to create a method within a parent or a superclass and then define the method in a subclass. Let's look at an example of this using Animal:

```
public class Dog extends Animal {
        public void makeSound() {
                System.out.println("Woof!");
}
public void makeSound (boleean   injured)
{
        if (injured) {

        System.out.println("Whimper");
        }
}
public class Cat extends Animal {
}
```

Let's say that we were able to create Animals. If you could, when you called makeSound() you would actually be calling the method that is defined within the superclass. If were to create a certain Dog, when you called makeSound() it would display "Woof!"; the same goes with Cat but, in this example, there is no `makeSound()` method so, when you call the method on Cat, it would be called within the Animal superclass and nothing would happen. Remember, because Cat and Dog both extend Animal, they are both subclasses of the Animal class.

This is known as Method Overriding and it is one of the most powerful parts of polymorphism. Java will allow this to happen because it is perfectly possible that specific object types have specific action behaviors. So, how does Java know which of the methods needs to be called> Java is always going to go for the true type of the object when it chooses whether to call the superclass or the subclass. In the next section, we will take about what true type means.

Dynamic Method Binding

Please, don't let this name scare you, it isn't that bad! We are not going to discuss dynamics but I will say this – Java will always determine which method is to be called, either at runtime or when your program is already running. Dynamic Method Binding is the method that Java uses to decide the method when it has to choose better the subclass and the superclass. But, how does Java decide? Before we can go into this, we must first look at the concept of true verso referenced type. Look at this example – we have created a Dog and declared it as Animal.

```
public static void main (String[] args) {
    Animal dog = new Dog();
}
```

Normally, this is what you would see:

```
public static void main (String[] args) {
    Dog dog = new Dog();
}
```

However, you are also able to declare variables by an abstract type or by their own supertype as a way of making things a bit more generic. Let's assume that you do not know the animal type that you want:

```
public static void main (String[] args) {
    Animal animal;
}
```

Did you notice that we haven't assigned the variable to anything? What we have here is an animal, not instantiated that equals nothing. We can't create only Animals because that would be abstract so we must specify the animal type. This is what we did in the previous example, creating the Animal as a new Dog.

So, in this example, which `makeSound()` version are you going to use in the case of `Animal animal = new Dog()`? Would you choose the version that goes with Dog or with Animal? The answer is that Java will do this for you by choosing the true type, the true type being the object that is being created. In the previous example, we have created a Dog even though we have used Animal as the reference to the variable.

So why wouldn't we just say `Dog dog = new Dog()`? The answer to that lies in abstraction – because we are using it we can group several different object types together. Let's look at an example of how this concept would be used for object storage:

```
public static void main (String[] args) {
        Animal dog = new Dog();
        Animal cat = new Cat();
        ArrayList<Animal>   animals   =   new
ArrayList<Animal>()
        animals.add(dog);
        animals.add(cat);
}
```

We simply couldn't do this if the Dog and Cat objects were created in the traditional manner and not referenced as Animals. What is important is that you don't confuse the true type and the reference. For example, you couldn't do this:

```
public static void main (String[] args) {
    Dog dog = new Animal();
}
```

First, you can't create objects in Animal as they are abstract. For the sake of simplicity, for a moment assume that you can do exactly that. It would still be classed as illegal because specific types are not able to be used as a reference to a broader type. Look at it in this way – dogs are animals but animals may not be dogs. What the above example says is, an Animal may be a Dog but this may not always be true.

Java polymorphism lets you control how objects are grouped and also allows you to make them as specific as they need to be. Polymorphism is also a vital part of object oriented programming because it allows you build object hierarchies – objects of a logical structure that make good sense in real-world examples. Polymorphism lets you write some pretty sophisticated Java programs that are very well-organized and incredibly easy to read. What it won't do is guarantee that your code is going to be awesome but, if you learn polymorphism and use it properly, you will certainly be well on your way.

As with every concept, your next step is to practice. Have a go at creating regular and abstract classes, object structures and have a go at making objects extend each other – note the results. Write the same method repeatedly using lots of different parameters; put them into the subclasses and the parent classes. Test your objects – write a main class that makes use of all the methods and the classes that you wrote in all those different ways.

If you can do all of that and learn from the results, you will be well on the way to mastering polymorphism

Chapter 6:
Variable Scope

You should be aware of variables by now, if not, go back to basic java and have a refresher on them before you continue. Now, if you do not understand the scope of a variable you will be a little confused on when you can use them. Think back to a piece of code where you might have seen the same variable name used in two separate places, each holding a different value. Think back to a time when you may have tried using a variable and the compiler has kicked off because you haven't referenced the variable in the context. This is down to variable scope and, hopefully, by the end of this chapter, you will be a little more enlightened in the mysteries of variable scope.

Class Level Scope

When you are writing Java code, there may be variables that you will need to access from anywhere inside a class. The variable scope has to be class level and there is only one way to create a class level variable in the class and outside of a method. Let's look at an example:

```
public class user {
      private String username
}
```

Did you spot that we defined the variables right at the top of the class before we defined any methods? This is a Java convention – class-level variables may be defined anywhere within a class as long as it is outside the methods of the class. It is, however, very good practice to have the variables right at the top simply so that you can see where they are. You should also have noted that the access identifier has nothing to do with the scope of the variable in the class. Again, if you are unsure of access identifiers, go back to basics and learn them again.

Method Scope

There are a few variables that you might want as temporary and they should only really be used in one method. This is method scope and the following is an example, using a Java main method, of a variable within method scope:

```
public static void main (String[] args) {
        int x = 5;

}
```

In the example, we have created variable x in the method. When the method has ended, the reference to the variable will disappear and you will not be able to access the variable again. You will not be able to use that variable x in any other method either because it will only exist in the scope of the main method. This is another example showing method scope but this time we have passed the variable in as a method parameter:

```
public void setName (String name) {
    username = name;
}
```

This is a typical setter method example and is a pretty good example. Now, let's look at this example again but this time, using a conflicting name for the variable:

```
private String username;
public void setName(String username) {
    this.username - username;
}
```

So, can you tell what is happening with the variable scope? And what on earth is "this"? The keyword "this" is used to help Java to tell the difference between the method, or local, scope variable and that variable in the class. "this.username" is telling Java that you want to reference the class variable. The setter is used to set "name", which is the method-scope variable, to the class variable of the same name. The scope of the variable is not conflicted because Java is able to work out which variable it needs to access, just through the "this" keyword. You can also do it this way:

```
private String username;
public void setName(String username) {
    username = this.username;
}
```

That said, this is not something you will do too often if you do it at all because you would be setting the temporary local variable to the value of the permanent variable.

Loop Scope

When you are dealing with `for` and `while` loops have you ever struggled to access a variable? Scope plays a huge role in this so let's look at what is going on.

Any variable that is created within a loop is local to that loop. What this means is that, when you exit out of the loop, that variable is no longer accessible. This will include any variables that may have been created in the signature of the loop. Look at the following examples of `for` loops:

Example 1:

```
public static void main (String[] args) {
        for (int x = 0; x = < 5; x++) {
                System.out.println("Loop    "   +
x);
        }
}
```

Example 2:

```
public static void main (String[] args) {
        int x;
```

```
for (x = 0; x < 5; x++) {
        System.out.println("Loop  "  +
x);
    }
}
```

In example 1, you can only use x inside the `for`
loop. In example 2, you can use x both inside
and outside the loop because it has been
declared outside, at method scope.

Generally speaking, sets of curly brackets {}
define a scope. In Java, you will normally be
able to access variables that are defined inside
of the same curly brackets as the code you have
written or the curly brackets that are within the
curly brackets where you defined the variable.

You should now have a better understanding of
the scope of variables in Java and now its time
for you to practice using them before you move
on.

Chapter 7: Logical Operators

Every single computer programming language includes logical operators, a way of expressing logic. Those in Java are split up into two different subtypes – conditional and relational. These can be used to make your computer code more flexible and definitely more powerful and you get the benefit of knowing that your code is so much easier to read and write.

Relational Operators

You should already know what relational operators are so I am just going to add the more advanced operators to the list you already have:

Operator	Meaning
==	is equal to
!=	is not equal to
>	is greater than
<	is less than
>=	is greater than or is equal to
<=	is less than or is equal to

Relational operators tend to be used mainly in `while` loops, `if` statements and, sometimes, `for` loops. These are the only uses. The one relational conditional which made be new is the "is not equal to" and this is what it will look like when used in an `if` statement:

```
if (num != 2) {
    //do stuff
}
```

The `if` statement will be true when the variable called `num` isn't equal to 2, otherwise the condition will return as true.

Conditional Operators

These are the conditional operators in Java

Operator
Meaning

Operator	Meaning
&&	AND
||	OR
!	NOT

Like the relational, conditional operators tend to be used only in `while` loops, `if` statements and `for` loops. The best way for me to show you these is to look at how they clean up your code.

And Operator

Let's assume that you want the program you write to output "You Win!" when num1 equals 3 and num2 equals 5:

```
if (num1 == 3) {
     if (num2 == 5)   {
          System.out.println("You
Win!");
     }
}
```

Java will go to the first `if` statement and if it is true, it will then move to the next `if` statement. If that is true as well it will then print `"You Win!"` on your screen. That should be simple enough but there is a much better way of placing one `if` statement inside another one. The answer to that lies in the AND operator:

```
if (num1 == 3 && num2 == 5) {
     System.out.println("You Win!");
}
```

Now that looks much better doesn't it.

Or Operator

Until now it has been stupidly hard to make several `if` statements that allow the code to be executed if one of the conditions is true. This is where the OR operator comes in, allowing your `if` statement to be true if just one out of a number of conditions can be met:

```
if (num1 == 3 || num2 == 5) {
     System.out.println("You Win!");
}
```

Can you see the difference between this code and the last one? This will only run if num1 equals 3 OR num2 equals 5. You only need one to be true but if both are then it will still work. The only time a false will be returned from the if statement is when both conditions are false.

To truly learn the logical operators, you need to understand logic and the best way for that is like this:

AND is when you everything must be true

OR is when you one thing needs to be true

There is one common mistake that tends to be made with the OR operator and Eclipse will kick out an error. Have a look at this code and see if you can figure it out:

```
if (num1 ==(3 || 4)) {
      System.out.println("You Win!");
}
```

Some people think that they can use parentheses to shorten their code but they can't. When you do this, Java hasn't a clue what you are talking about and will simply throw an error out. Remember – Java will always execute the code that is within a set of parentheses first. In the above example, it will see 3 or 5 and doesn't know what it all means. Make sure you always use the OR operator correctly

Not Operator

This is the easiest of them all to learn because it is nothing more than the opposite of what the code is saying:

```
if ( !(num1 ==3)  )  {
    System.out.println("You Win!");
}
```

Note that there is an extra parenthesis set. What the `if` statement is saying here is that if NOT num1 equals 3 – basically, if num1 isn't equal to 3. Can you see how that will work? Have a bit of practice and see how it works. One more thing; had you spotted that the "is not equal to" statement seems a bit familiar?

```
if ( num1 != 3 )  {
    System.out.println("You Win!");
}
```

This the same and this is a much easier way to use the "is not equal to" statement and it is more readable.

This is a better example of how to use the not operator by itself:

```
boolean flag = true;
if (!flag) {
     system.out.println("You Win!");
}
```

Ok, let's just back up for a minute. First, we have used a boolean variable here and have set it as true. Next comes the if statement – remember, flag is equal to true so, if you translate that to English, rather than saying "if not flag" it actually says "if not true". But how will this work?

What is happening here is that "if not true" wants to know if the flag variable isn't true, or is false. If it is false, Java will print "You Win!" Because we have set flag to true, that won't happen. Have a go at removing the NOT operator and seeing what happens when you run the code – Java displays "You Win!" because the if statement is now looking to see if flag is true.

Order of Logical Operators

All logical operators have an operation order to follow and this is very important when you begin mixing and matching your operators. AND will always happen before OR and the only way to make them happen in a different order in Java is through the use of parentheses. Look at this example:

```
int num1 = 3;
int num2 = 5;
int num3 = 7;
if ( num1 == 9 && num2 == 2 || num3 == 7
) {
        System.out.println("You Win!");

}
```

Think about this code carefully and what you think is going to happen. Is Java going to print "You Win!"? Remember the logic.

If num1 equals 9 AND num2 equals 2 OR num3 equals 7.

You could say that as num1 isn't equal to 9 the remainder of the statement is irrelevant and Java will not print "You Win!"

You would be wrong I'm afraid.

As Java reads from left to right, strictly, this is what is really going to happen:

Java will look at the first and second conditions. If num1 equals 9 AND num2 equals 2. It will then decide that neither of these is true so it then goes to the OR operator. Java will then determine if either side of the operator is true and, as num3 does equal 7, it will print "You Win!" What Java did was combined conditions one and two and then compared them to the other side of the OR operator. To get the result we thought it would be, you would need to place the OR bit inside parentheses:

```
int num1 = 3;
int num2 = 5;
int num3 = 7;
if ( num1 == 9 && (num2 == 2 || num3 == 7
)) {
        System.out.println("You Win!");
}
```

Now you won't see anything displayed.

Until you are comfortable with using the logical operators and with the logic that dictates them, use parentheses as often as you can – in the right places. This will ensure that you don't end up confused about the way the logic gets grouped.

With any luck, this has all made sense and you can start using logical operators straightaway. They are very useful and will let you come up with better programs. Have a go at experimenting with the logical operators so that you understand them better.

Bonus Chapter: The J2EE Environment

J2EE uses Java 2 Platform Standard Edition (J2SE) as the basis to build on, providing services that are needed to build applications that are:

- Large scale
- Distributed
- Component based
- Multi-tier

In essence, J2EE is a set of APIs that are used to build these systems although that is just half of it. J2EE is the standard used for the build and deployment of enterprise applications all glued together by the API specifications that are defined and the services provided by J2EE. In other words, the "Write once, run anywhere" promise from Java will apply in enterprise applications as well. This means that enterprise applications may run on different platforms so long as they support the Java 2 platform. These applications are portable between all application servers that support J2EE specifications.

What Does J2EE Comprise of?

J2EE comprises many different APIs that are used to build these enterprise applications. Although the API list might seem a little overwhelming to start with, do keep in mind that some of them are used primarily by the

J2EE environment that your application executes in while other provide services that may not be required by your application. It is worth keeping in mind that you don't need all of them to build your J2EE application but, for the sake of clarity, the technology list that makes up J2EE is:

- Java Servlets
- JavaServer Pages (JSP)
- Enterprise JavaBeans (EJB)
- Java Message Service (JMS)
- Java Naming and Directory Interface (JNDI)
- Java Database Connectivity (JDBC)
- JavaMail
- Java Transaction Service (JTS)
- Java Transaction API (JTA)
- J2EE Connector Architecture (J2EE-CA, or JCA)

From the perspective of a developer, the primary technologies to use are:
- EJB – Enterprise JavaBeans
- JSP – JavaServer Pages
- Java Servlets
- JDBC – Java Database Connectivity
- JMS – Java Messaging Service

On occasion, JNDI (Java Naming and Directory Interface) is used as a way of locating

EJBs (Enterprise JavaBeans), along with other resources for the enterprise.

Java Servlets

At the highest level, a Java Servlet is the Java equivalent of a CGI script and those are used to process and service client requests that come through a web server. From the perspective of implementation, a servlet is nothing more than a Java class that is able to implement a class that has been predefined.

One of the main uses for a servlet is to dynamically generate content that is to be presented to the user and this is done through markup language being embedded in the Java code. An example of this would be HTML. As a servlet is written in Java it will have full access to the Java features libraries and that includes being able to access enterprise resources and databases.

JavaServer Pages

JSP is used to present information to a user over the internet and makes use of a model whereby Java code will be embedded in HTML – the opposite of what the servlet does. JS Pages are written as files in HTML and contain embedded code called scriptlets.

One of the downfalls of JSP is that you can easily build up big pages full of embedded code and logic and this is why JSP can easily be integrated with JavaBeans and something else called JSP tag extensions. These are custom tags or custom actions that allow for functionality that can be re-used to be placed inside XML-like tags and these can be reused on pages by designers and developers alike.

What are Enterprise JavaBeans?

These are a large part of J2EE specifications and they define the model for server-side building – components that are reusable. There are three types of beans that have support in J2EE:

Session Beans: these are extensions to client applications and tend to be used as a way of modeling business processes. There are two different session beans – stateless and stateful. Stateless session beans can be shared between several clients at a time while stateful beans tend to be used to record a conversational state for one client.

Entity Beans: these are used as a way of modeling persistent business bodies, more specifically data that is in a database. One of the more common mappings is to model one of the entity beans on a table with there being one bean (one instance) for each row in this table. Persistence may be achieved in one of two ways – bean managed and container managed persistence. With container-managed persistence, mapping will be defined at the time of deployment between the table columns and the persistent properties within the bean. With bean-managed persistence, the developer will write JBDC code that will perform several operations – create, read, update and delete.

Message-Driven Beans: these allow for functionality execution on a non-parallel basis and are usually triggered by JMS messages that come from middleware that is message-oriented.

What is JMS?

JMS is one of the Java APIs that presents interfaces into middleware that is message-oriented. Examples of these would be MQSeries, IBM, SonicMQ and others like them. Similar to JDBC, JMS will give a Java application the mechanism needed to integrate with these systems. It does this by providing a common program interface regardless of what the underlying system for messaging. In functional terms, JMS lets messages be received and sent using Publish/Subscribe or point to point models.

Running a J2EE Application

There are three steps to running any J2EE application:

- Build
- Package
- Deploy

Step one is to build the application. J2EE has the support of lots of different tools, open sure and commercial and these are incredibly useful in taking away a certain amount of the complexity that surrounds development

Step two, once your application is built, is to package it. The packaging will be determined by the type of J2EE component you used to build the application. Basically, though, all you are doing is packing up all the components and the classes into an archive file, such as JAR. As well as containing the compiled code, you will also need to use deployment descriptors to configure some of the characteristics that go with some components. These are XML fields, used to describe how a particular component behaves when it is run in a J2EE environment.

The last step is deployment. Because J2EE is a collection of specifications and APIs, an application server has to be installed – this is the software that will implement the specifications and will provide all of the services that the components need to run.

And, I am going to leave that there, J2EE is a lot more complex that Java, even advanced Java so this is just a basic overview of what it is, rather than an in-depth discussion on how to use it.

Conclusion

Thank you again for downloading this book!

I hope this book was able to help you to improve and advance your Java programming knowledge.

The next step is, quite simply, to practice and keep on practicing and advancing your knowledge. Like anything, if you don't keep up with Java, keep up with all the latest developments, then you will fall behind and will find yourself having to start all over again – the very last thing that you want.

There are plenty of online resources, including support forums, courses and training help that you can refer to. One of the best ways is to join the support forums – here you will find plenty of help and support and can ask any question you may have.

Finally, if this book has given you value and helped you in any way, then I'd like to ask you for a favor, if you would be kind enough to leave a review for this book on Amazon? It'd be greatly appreciated!

Thank you and good luck!

About the Author

Charlie Masterson is a computer programmer and instructor who have developed several applications and computer programs.

As a computer science student, he got interested in programming early but got frustrated learning the highly complex subject matter.

Charlie wanted a teaching method that he could easily learn from and develop his programming skills. He soon discovered a teaching series that made him learn faster and better.

Applying the same approach, Charlie successfully learned different programming languages and is now teaching the subject matter through writing books.

With the books that he writes on computer programming, he hopes to provide great value and help readers interested to learn computer-related topics.

www.ingramcontent.com/pod-product-compliance
Lightning Source LLC
Chambersburg PA
CBHW071107050326
40690CB00008B/1139